DON'T

DIET

Fran Hornsby

AuthorHouse™ UK Ltd.
500 Avebury Boulevard
Central Milton Keynes, MK9 2BE
www.authorhouse.co.uk
Phone: 08001974150

First published by AuthorHouse 12/18/2008

ISBN: 978-1-4389-3890-5 (sc)

Printed in the United States of America
Bloomington, Indiana

This book is printed on acid-free paper.

Don't

D epend on

I deas from

E xternal sources

T hink for yourself.

'Our life is a as a result of our thinking. If we can understand and be aware of that thinking then we can change our life for the better anytime we choose!'

For the reader of this book, may you have the success in taking charge of your life and in believing you are OK.

May you change enough to let go of the struggle with food and let go of your weight both in the physical sense and in the psychological sense.

I dedicate this book to my children, who without knowing have supported the beliefs in this book and have proven that when these messages are given at an early enough age, a harmonious relationship with food can be sustained and weight does not have to be a battle.

"W8 4Life" is a program that supports this work and can facilitate the reader through this journey.

Look at the website: www.w8-4life.co.uk

Why Has This Book Been Written?

I will keep this introduction brief, as I am sure you will want to get on with reading this book and discover how it can help you.

My background, and the background to this book, is my profession as a person-centred therapist, a therapist with a particular interest in weight loss. I take ownership of every decision that I have made, although the decisions have not always been obvious ones to me at the time.

I am now able to realise that with each decision taken I have been travelling a path that has brought me to a point whereby I now feel wholly dedicated and passionate about what I do.

So... I have spent twenty years in the medical profession, assisting and giving anaesthetics whilst patients undergo surgery. Towards the end of that time I took five years to train as a Rogerian counsellor, with the desire to move away from the medical profession and move into the psychological area of life and set up my own private practice, using the skills I had learnt. Eventually, I set up my practice, initially running programmes based on a food-abstinence regime complimented by therapeutic counselling. Through this, I began to understand more and more how people relate to food and to issues around weight loss. I subsequently developed therapy groups which did not rely on food abstinence and which constituted an intervention that I found I was good at delivering. This work utilised both Transactional Analysis and Cognitive Behavioural Therapy, which are other schools of therapy that I have also become extremely knowledgeable in.

The steep learning curve for me has been to recognise wholeheartedly that all institutions involved in the 'slimming' business – including the food-abstinence diet that I am now not a part of for reasons of professional integrity – absolutely miss the point. This is high-lighted for me when I meet people who have been a part of those institutions for the best part of their lives and hear them recite the messages drilled into them: 'That's a free food' and 'That food is a sin'.

These messages actually work against long-term weight loss and weight management, and those institutions have damaged the individual and blocked them from seeing food as 'just' food, something to truly enjoy and needed for nutrition. A wedge gets driven between food and the person, which results in dysfunctional thinking, and therefore behaviour, and consequently causes acute damage to the individual.

I had not really focussed on weight or food relationships before. However, I have suffered from being the largest in my family, a family of three girls and a mother and father. Also, in my pubescent years I bordered on having anorexia nervosa and weighed as low as 6 stone weight.

To date, I have spent eight years seeing clients in my practice, clients who present with all types of issues. Particularly, though, I see clients for whom food, eating, and being overweight appear to be the presenting issues, when in fact they are merely symptomatic of issues deep within them.

Furthermore therapeutic counselling, and not dieting, is needed to overcome the problems that arise from these issues.

It soon becomes apparent that counselling provides the liberation and offers the choice to let go of this area of obsession and overcome the weight.

Accordingly, this book recognises that the issue is not about food, but about us. Our relationship with food is merely reflective of our relationship with life. This book invites you on a journey, during which you will be prompted to look at many things, including a search deep into your inner self. Throughout the book you will be introduced to the concepts underpinning Transactional Analysis and Cognitive Behavioural Therapy. You will also be introduced to what are called the Parent, Adult, and Child ego states within all of us.

We will consider the origins of our relationship with food.

Why do we over-consume? It will become evident that food enables behaviour. We will look at the behaviours that food enables, what type of behaviour it enables, and why. We will examine different types of behaviour, ranging from routine to habitual to addictive.

We will investigate the presenting reasons that cause us to overeat and explore the underlying assumptions that keep us stuck in our life.

We will look at our 'personality type', one that when extreme is not helpful to us, and we will consider how to lessen the strength of that personality type so that we can be in harmony with ourselves. We will consider our extreme thinking about food and the idea that there are 'good" and 'bad' foods. In other words, we will examine the distorted thinking we impose on food and its connection with our personality type.

We will be introduced to the concept of being kinder to ourselves around food and learn where we need to go and where we need to be with ourselves for food to be in its place.

We will find the tools to facilitate recovery for those of us who have battled and then been beaten by the demons around food and weight.

At times, this book might seem complicated and rather removed from the subject of food and/or fat, but by the end you will the understand why success has evaded you. It will give you the tools to help keep your weight off, along with explaining why you might have had to stay fat in the past.

Keep this in mind throughout: 'It is not what you eat, but it is who you are!'

The under pinning fact is always: 'Food enables behaviour!'

Chapter One

FOOD AND BEHAVIOUR

We Have Inherited a Relationship with Food.

From a very early age we were given messages about food from our parents, usually our mums or grandmothers.

Certain foods were offered to us, in essence, as bribes or as treats or even as something that would make us feel better. These foods were given a meaning that bore no relation to their real properties. The messages that introduced these distorted beliefs sounded like this: 'If you're a good girl, you can have a biscuit.' 'Eat everything up – we mustn't waste food – and then you can have dessert.' 'Does your knee hurt? Never mind, you'll be alright – here, have some chocolate buttons.' Now I have started I'm sure you can now remember many more.

Our parents heard these messages from their parents, and if we sit and really think about this, we realise that their lives and their relationship with food have been markedly affected by World Wars One and Two.

Their relationship with food was and still is very different than ours, and the attitudes they have to it are the product of its scarcity in their younger life. The amount of food available during either war was restricted, and to acquire food necessitated having a ration book. Even then only foods such as rice, potatoes, bread, and some basic vegetables were the only food stuffs that were most frequently acquired through this system. Meat was hard to come by, and people bartered the basic foodstuffs to get a little more tea, flour, sugar, and eggs – luxuries to be served as a treat, such as cakes and buns with tea. It was important that everyone ate what they were given. After all, there really was no more where that came from, and the mums and dads had scrimped and saved, not only money but other goods, to feed their families.

The body needed food to survive, so whether our parents and grandparents actually liked the food they ate did not come into the equation.

There was definitely no more where that came from, and to eat it was a necessity.

I always remember working with an elderly lady who thought a mashed potato sandwich was the perfect treat. For those generations that had either lived through the wars or for whose lives had been affected by someone else whom had been directly influenced by the wars they would experience food becoming less scarce. However by now these generations had been greatly affected by the hungry days they had lived through and had deep set beliefs that food was to be valued and not wasted.

As this generation grew up, so wages rose and people could afford to buy more food, but by then food had become categorised into certain groups. It had always been a precious commodity and still needed to be stretched as far as possible. Many a mum would spend the day baking so that those luxuries of cakes and scones could be around in the home but without being too expensive. Roast on Sunday would be followed on Monday by soup made from the leftover meat and bones, or bubble and squeak made from the leftover vegetables. Food could not be thrown away. Even after rationing ended, the message was, 'What about those starving people in Africa? Really, we must not waste.' So whether they liked it or not, our parents and grandparents had to eat it all up.

The matriarch of the family was very much in charge of the food and controlled when it was eaten, both in quantity and in the food type, it was offered to the rest of the family in a very systematic pattern involving the set meal times of breakfast lunch and tea, in order that it would last the whole week. As mentioned before the Sunday baking of cakes and scones was often done on Sunday and expected to last until the following Sunday, when the next batch would be baked. For the cakes and buns to last for a whole week, consumption had to be controlled, making them a precious treat.

As a child, I spent many a day picking currants and berries from bushes in the fields and by the roadside, and going into orchards where we could pick our own fruit. These were ways of gaining precious fruits to make the pies that would be served with custard as special desserts. Many of us have memories of grannies always having wonderfully sweet apple pie with milky custard.

Desserts were seen as a symbol of successful food management, if the dessert was wholesome it appeared to represent the mum as a 'good mum', a granny as a 'good granny', and then there would be the 'good wife'. Mothers worked hard to provide well-balanced meals. To have a pudding – a pie with custard – after the ordinary main course meant that the pudding would have been made from scratch, and time would have been spent making it. The effort that went into making it would indicate the equal measure of nurturing and caring. Often a mother offered dessert as the treat she didn't have as a child. There was a sense of pride and accomplishment in feeding the family. As there was so much at stake mothers budgeted strictly, to be sure they could provide. Food was shared with a tight control, with restrictions making some foods more valuable than others.

All this helps us begin to understand the origins of our thoughts about food and to recognise their inappropriateness in today's society, where we have food in abundance. We can now see that we need to adopt a different attitude to food, so our relationship with it ceases to be dysfunctional for us.

The origins of our relationship.

Let's look at our relationship with food.

There is a definite difference in how we view certain foods, and dependant on how they have been offered to us our relationship will reflects the messages we heard in childhood.

We see the crisps, cakes, and chocolate, or even chips and 'take a ways' – and in some cases bread as 'yummy' foods. These have been restricted, or offered with a sense that they are in some way precious. Tight control made them special, so we turn to them when we believe we deserve a treat. A treat that has been created by increasing its value caused by its short supply

Now, let's look at the messages wrapped around these foods: 'Be a good girl and you can have a sweetie.' 'Sit quietly and you can have a packet of crisps.' 'Well done, that was great, have a bar of chocolate.' 'Let's cuddle up and watch a movie and have some popcorn.' 'We'll take a break and have a nice cup of tea and a piece of cake.'

These comments and many others underlie the comfort we get from these foods. They suggest warmth, and love and cuddles, and they also suggest reward. After all, we were never offered a piece of broccoli for being good or for keeping quiet – our parents never saw those foods as special.

Today we live under the influence of such messages. At the same time, we have such an abundance of all foods that food treats are no longer scarce. We can, if we like, have Christmas dinner every day of the year; we can eat Wimbledon strawberries and cream year round; and we can buy chocolate Easter eggs in January.

Authorities on dieting reinforce unhelpful messages by segregating food into categories. We are told that we can have one 'sin' a day, or that Jaffa cakes are a 'free' food, and so on. Yet food is just food, meant to replenish the energy we expend.

I hear you saying, 'If only that could be the case!'

It can be. We don't want to end the pleasure of eating – it is an immensely enjoyable pastime…when it doesn't affect us badly and produce results we really hate.

Now that we're beginning to gain clarity and understanding as to why we think as we do around food we can see how strongly the relationship past generations had with food shapes and influences our thoughts today, and how those thoughts distort the very essence of why we believe we need to eat, as well as inhibit our real enjoyment of food.

How the Brain Affects What We Think about Food

Let's look at a simplified picture of the brain, at the parts that are important for understanding our relationship with food.

The Chief Executive (dorsolateral prefrontal cortex): The CE co-ordinates our awareness of what is going on. He plans, and makes decisions, and forms our expectations of what is going to happen.

The Personal Assistant (anterior cingulate): When the PA is efficient she keeps the wheels of the operation turning and makes common-sense decisions without bothering the boss. This will involve everything we do without conscious thought. So when the PA is in charge the CE is out to lunch!
The Filing Cabinet (hippocampus): This is our conscious memory store and holds all our important memories.

The Guardsman (amygdala): This guardsman stores our unconscious emotional memories and conditioned responses. He acts on them and identifies for us whether our experiences are new or familiar and responds accordingly.

So we have four main actors of the brain. Let us apply them to a specific scenario so that we are able to understand the `workings` that occur.

We come in from work and, as usual, want to eat that special something. After all, we have worked hard today and we feel we are deserving of a little treat, and a treat helps us unwind. But today we have decided to restrict our 'picky' foods because we want to lose some weight, and it does not serve us well to eat when we come straight from work and then also have our evening meal. This behaviour leads to gaining weight, and we also feel quite full and bloated for the evening, not to mention the guilt that builds within us.

So the Chief Executive sends down a message informing us that we are not going to eat any more at this time of day for the near future. We respond and consequently resist the urge we have from habit-formed behaviour and do not eat.

However, the resistance does not go unnoticed. We do experience feelings of withdrawal. We also very much believe we are being 'hard done by' and notice the loss of those yummy 'picky' foods. The withdrawal symptom we physiologically experience is relatively mild at this stage – it may be a faint nagging feeling, or a slight sensation in the mouth or stomach, similar to a mild hunger pang. But being determined to cut down this particular time in the day, we successfully resist the desire to eat at this moment.

By the time nine 'clock comes, however, and all we have eaten is the 'good' food meal, which probably contained very low levels of carbohydrates and a complete absence of sugars, the hypothalamus – a structure in our brain that monitors the levels of 'food chemicals' such as carbohydrates – indicates that carbohydrate levels are below normal, so it sends out an alert to the Guardsman to say 'Top up on the carbs.'

In addition to the physiology, our psychology delivers us beliefs about our virtuousness: what angels we have been not to have had any of 'those' food types. There is often a deeper thought – that we have a few 'brownie' points in hand because we have not snacked when we arrived home from work, and if we analysed the day more, we have probably not eaten at all during the day, because we have worked so hard and it has been so busy ... So the odds are mounting as to whether we can continue along this 'path of good behaviour with food

If that is not enough to defeat our attempt to restrict our intake of 'picky' foods, there is the very familiar experience of going to bed feeling awful, feeling over--full, and thinking how once again we have failed, and being very remorseful over the never-ending cycle of habitual behaviour.

Getting back to the physiology, we see that sending this message from the hypothalamus to the Guardsman will in itself trigger yet another mild withdrawal symptom!

The Guardsman will be in full agreement with the message that the carb levels are meant to be higher than they are, and consequently will assume the Chief Executive has got it wrong when he said no carbs at this time.

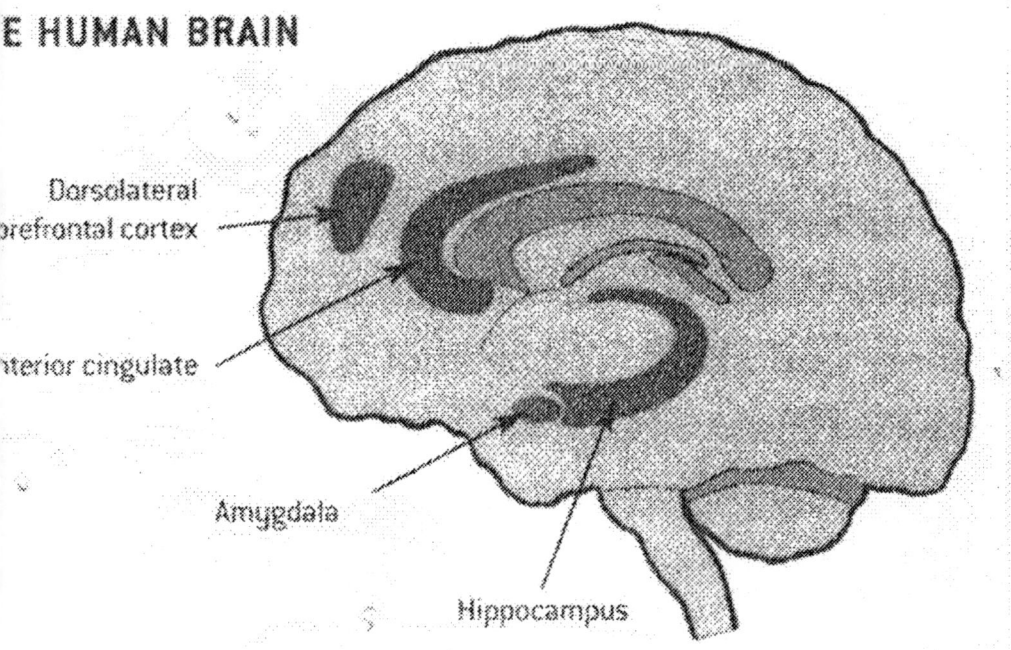

E HUMAN BRAIN

Dorsolateral
prefrontal cortex

nterior cingulate

Amygdala

Hippocampus

So the Guardsman begins to gather in agreement from other areas and attempts to persuade the PA to convince the Chief Executive that he has got this 'no carb' situation all wrong.

As he gains momentum and convinces these people that he is right, a chemical called dopamine is secreted in the brain. Dopamine is the 'fight or flight' chemical, and as its levels become higher, we are charged more and more to react. Dopamine spurs us to take action! In this particular instance, the message is definitely high priority. As you can imagine, food is so important to us that our levels of dopamine become very high.

Rather than panic, instantly the PA, who often receives such messages, will automatically feel the need to put this into context, rather then blindly react, and gain some sense of priority. To do this, she looks into the Filing Cabinet, to find out if there is any validity to these messages and to see if there have been other similar situations in the past.

She finds many files of memories connected with eating – especially to the enjoyment of eating when we come home from work. In full, when we eat those particular foods we remember the happy times.

Historically, we have experienced that these foods make us better, make us feel loved and grant us reward. After all, when we were children this is how they were offered!

So when the PA receives these clips from the Filing Cabinet, she is alarmed by the realization of how enjoyable this has been, and immediately alerts the Chief Executive to facts that he must have got this decision all wrong, and surely he must want for us to eat these foods now.

Let us imagine that our PA really is startled by the conflict between the Chief Executive's decision and what the Filing Cabinet files reveal. The amount of surprise – and therefore the desire to influence the Chief Executive into taking an alternative action – is very strong.

The strength of this interaction dictates the levels of dopamine produced, so at this point the levels are very, very high, and we are so charged by this chemical that we have no alternative but to eat the food types we have so tried to avoid.

It would be very easy for us to now feel extremely disheartened. How can we control the levels of dopamine in our brain? We must be on a 'hiding' to nothing! Let us keep calm; we always have choice.

The most powerful weapon at our disposal in the fight against this habitual behaviour and this production of dopamine is our *expectation*.

Expectations are fundamental in life. Through our experiences, we learn what to expect: expectations are resources that enable us to help ourselves get our needs met. We live with constant expectations, some based on reality, and others made up from assumptions that are distorted (these we shall look at later):

- When it rains, we expect to get wet.

- If we don't eat, we expect to feel hungry.

- If we touch a flame, we expect to get burnt.

Then there are the more complex expectations that involve our interactions with other people. Our experiences have taught us that:

- If we shout at someone, then we will expect that other person to give us an unfavourable response, which could be one of many reactions, for instance, they could shout back, or they could walk away or even that the other person could hurt us. The expectation is not so clear-cut, for us as it does depend on the other person.

- If we hit someone, then that someone could either hit back, or they might shout at us or once again they could walk away.

On the whole, we have a choice of expectations, learnt from out our experiences, and we often find that we place them as either 'negative' or as 'positive expectations.

Linked into our expectations are our emotions.

Emotions arise from our thoughts, and expectations are a type of thought.

Emotions always arise from the expectations we have and follow on from the 'pattern matching' produced by the Guardsman.

We think about something, and construct an expectation around that scenario, based on our experience. From that expectation, we understand what to do, and we 'do' that something.

It is our emotions – arising from what we 'do', from the different expectations that we have – that drive us to experience such a wonderful varied emotional life.

Unfortunately we are not aware of this for the most part and believe that emotions make us too unstable to manage.

If we look at the origin of the word 'emotions' we will see that the word is derived from the Latin *'emovere'*, which means to move outwards and to stir up.

So emotions, too, produce an urge to take some sort of action. Emotions always arise from our expectations and are the result of the pattern-matching made by the Guardsman.

Let us look at some examples that will support this:

- When we are happy, we laugh; we like to celebrate and enjoy life not only on our own but with others as well.

- When we feel desire and are attracted to another, we want to get close to them and feel their warmth, and want to entice and seduce them.

- When feeling sad, we often want to withdraw and be alone, as we also feel vulnerable and scared.

- Anger can sometimes be physically felt; it is a high energy emotion if felt in its fullness, and there is often a desire to shout, to be loud, and on occasion we feel an urge to physically let go of the energy, so we might smash a plate.

(It might be the case that you read this and think that this is not you. For those of you that do not agree with this, your disagreement will be a result of your fear of what being angry might have you do, so you internalise it and will be the absolute opposite: you will be quite still and motionless. This is not to say that you are not angry; you deal with it in a way that makes you unable to really contact that emotion.)

- To feel disgusted about something will have us make a face and want to get right away from the thing that disgusts us. We do not like what we see and want to keep ourselves safe from whatever it is.

Our emotions are a result of our learned expectations, and they are our driving force.

A more detailed example would be: We are doing something outside. It is lovely and warm, and we are with our friends, so the expectation will be that of enjoying the situation. We will expect the occasion to be a nice one, and so we will feel happy, warm, and comfortable. We have expectations about that situation and thus will have certain emotions.

I'm sure that when we have experienced ourselves being irritable, that in itself makes us cross, because it does not fit in with our expectation of having a good time during a social gathering.

We expect to feel happy when we eat carbohydrates, because our experiences of old have given us the evidence to back this belief up When we eat our 'picky' foods we remember those times as being good times. The chocolate, or the crisps, or whatever takes us back to moments of 'heaven'! This feeds into the baggage we have that 'picky' foods are the foods that create a sense of everything being great, even if it wasn't a minute ago.

Therefore, we can see that the Guardsman has the power to trigger, to initiate, levels of dopamine, from the expectations we have, but he does not have the emotional intelligence to instigate any emotional subtleties.

The emotions have to be triggered by the PA.

Hold on, we are nearly there!

So to stop the cravings for the food, to stop those thoughts in our head of needing food when we return home from work – which therefore initiates high levels of dopamine being produced – we have to look at the way we think, the psychology.
We have to check out the expectations that we have linked to the food we believe 'takes over' and the behaviour we have become caught up in.

We always want to 'do' something, so our emotions are very closely linked to a set of expectations. This set of expectations represents the memo given by the Guardsman to the PA.

We need to appreciate, however, that the Guardsman only has the power to trigger the dopamine release from the information given by the hypothalamus, the part of our brain that just measures the levels of chemicals in our blood. He does not have the ability to instigate the emotional intelligence involved with our expectations; that has to be done by the PA, who relies upon the memories we choose to give her from our Filing Cabinet.

If we can stay with the mild cravings produced at the physiological level – the point when the Guardsman acts on the message from the hypothalamus – we will survive the experience without having to give in.

But if we let those mild cravings reach the psychological level – the level where the PA adds so much dopamine to the persuasive messages, because we choose to keep hold of expectations that embrace 'glorious' thoughts around us eating 'picky' foods – then our ability to withdraw will be non-existent.

The key word here is 'let'. Our expectations decide the strength of the dopamine, and our thoughts have the power to decide what expectations to have.

Let's look at our scenario: Our expectation is that eating when we arrive home is an enjoyable experience and one that makes us happy. We almost protect the thought that those foodstuffs we choose to eat at that time do, honestly make us feel better. After all, we have been brought up with the belief that those foods make us better; they are a treat to us, and after a day at work we do so want a treat for getting through the day.

These memories in the Filing Cabinet are, however – when looked into in further detail – distorted. In fact, they are almost false, because most of the experiences recalled and sent on up to the PA, in one way never really happened.

The reality of eating, gorging upon arriving home after a day's work is that we feel really annoyed with ourselves. Every time we eat when we come home – in that tense and quite driven moment – we almost instantly wished we had not. We always chose the 'junk'-type of foods, the easy-to-grab type of foods, as we see them as the treat. Unfortunately, they are the calorie-heavy foods, and the type of foods that when we eat quickly will result in eating larger quantities than is appropriate and therefore result in weight gain. Consequently, we instantly wish we had not fallen into this behaviour pattern yet again, because once more we have become too full and then had to eat the evening meal. Whilst eating it all the time wishing that we were not so full from all those 'picky' and high-fat foods. The remorse each time, the feelings of guilt and disappointment in ourselves because of the fallen attempt not to engage with this behaviour pattern, is the true experience, and the true expectation and emotional experience in regard to this particular behaviour.

If we go back to our original example, our expectations around eating carbs are that something really wonderful is going to happen. We truly believe that we love those food types, and when we take that first mouthful we think we are in heaven.

We experience joy and relaxation along with many other emotions. We also expect that these feelings can continue, if we continue to eat. So we take another bite, because we want more of the same bit of heaven. However, with every bite, our physiology realises the levels of chemicals are fine, if not becoming too high, and so wants us to stop. Our psychology starts to take over, stubbornly, because 'we want heaven', and we definitely remember that in days of old we had heaven when we ate these types of food in this way!

Realistically, however, what now happens is that with the amount we eat and the inappropriateness of when we eat, the sense of satisfaction and stimulation is never totally delivered by the food. It cannot be because it is only food.

So we trick ourselves into this selective recall from the Guardsman and the Filing Cabinet. He is only given the expectation that we felt when we were children and were given treats by the people we loved, and in 'correct' quantities and at controlled, appropriate times. These files keep us trapped into doing things for the wrong reasons, because of euphoric recall.

Around the food issue, we choose to continue with this euphoric recall; we hold on to this expectation that particular foods make us feel better. This will always result in dopamine being constantly discharged at high levels, which forces us to then do something, which in this case will lead to eating.

Yet all that happens from the increased levels of dopamine is that we buy ourselves a cheap trance state, a way of being, 'out of –it' for a very little while, because while we are eating those foods we allow ourselves to think of nothing but the apparent joy of the food. As we all know, however, we swallow the food and instantly wish we never had. The remorse and the guilt stay with us for nearly the rest of the day.

We become confused, because we still choose to have only old memories, memories that belonged to us as children, memories of how we experienced these foods in different times. In that confusion, our psychology struggles to realise the expectations and therefore continues to persuade the Chief Executive that it is a good idea to continue with the same behaviour, with the foods of old.

The amount of dopamine that is generated deceives us into expecting that we will experience the heaven we want, as long as we continue in the rut that we are used to. And so the perpetual illusion is maintained, and we still hold on to that expectation.

All that stops our behaviour is either we physiologically feel sick, or that, psychologically, the present hits us and we feel guilty, lethargic, angry, and hopeless.

By staying realistic and living more in the present we would realise that the memories we hold and choose to recollect around the food types are completely distorted and that what we do today is very different from back then.

In fact, most of the good experiences recalled and sent on up to the PA never really happened, because when we eat carbohydrates now, either in large quantities or at inappropriate times, we feel lethargic, guilty, and basically quite horrid.

In truth, what we do is cheat ourselves; our selective recall – euphoric recall – keeps us trapped. We remember when the behaviour was introduced to us and the circumstances, and consequently how it made us feel better. Through time, however, we have distorted these experiences in many ways, and the reality of the distorted behaviour is over-shadowed by the memories.

All dopamine does is buy us a cheap trance state – a way of being out of it- for a while, which enables us to avoid facing the fact that our true needs are not being met!

Euphoric recall gives us a momentary metaphorical hug, which in itself enables us to avoid facing the fact that our true needs are not being met.

What Does Your Behaviour Do For You?

1. How and why did you start it? (think about the behaviour in itself and the foods that enable that behaviour.)

2. What do you enjoy about it? (about eating at that time and eating those foods.)

3. How your portion size of food and frequency of eating has changed over time?

4. What it is you like about this behaviour pattern now?

5. What good experiences you have had in the past with this behaviour? had with it?

So now we begin to realise how we really do use food as a mechanism to indulge old behaviours and belief systems that we inherited from previous generations and that do not belong in today's culture. However, the behaviour itself enables us to divert our attention from other issues and use food and our weight problems to continue to avoid facing the fact that our own true needs are not being met.

We see food as everything it is not; we see it as something that can give us a lift, a happy pill, something that can love us, care for us, make us feel better when we are down. And yet food is just food.

The hypothalamus registers food as just food, but the psychological side of us interrupts and over-rides that. We have it all mixed up, and so the carrot cannot be seen in the same way as the chocolate!

When did we last eat food for the simple reason – the appropriate reason – of hunger?

Let us now look at the distorted reasoning we have around food, the beliefs that come from our inherited relationship with food, and how the messages that we grew up with have affected us.

We have over-consumed and do over-consume for the following reasons:

Management of our emotions

- Anger
- Stress/Anxiety
- Sadness
- Frustration
- Boredom
- Irritation
- Tiredness… and any other emotion that we can think of.

Then there are the associative behaviours:

- Because the food is there

- We cannot waste it

- We have to finish the food on our plate

- To socialise with others

- To feel the same as others, to feel 'normal'

- We have just come home from work

- It's Friday and the end of the week

The list is long; we could probably add to it now that we have some insight into the type of reasoning we use.

Hunger is not amongst these reasons; we do not eat food for the real reasons that it is present on earth, but for something else.

That 'something else' is that food enables behaviour.

As we sow this seed, food enables behaviour, and as we introduce different ways of thinking about food, we need to move away from the ingrained belief that we so love actual food. Frequently, at first meeting, clients in my practice were adamant that they 'loved' food, and I was not to persuade them away from that belief.

Well, yes, I guess we rather believe that we do love food. However, if we were to apply this dynamic to another example, such as really loving the rain , it would be totally acceptable to make that statement when the land is a little arid or at least dry. However, if the land were soaked with water, or maybe flooded, we would question that statement, wouldn't we?

Eating for any reason other then hunger results in us feeding into our euphoric recall. The stimulation from, or satisfaction of, eating food because of hunger is never experienced, and yet this is the true 'use' of food. So when we eat and are not hungry, it is like rain pouring onto a soaked land; the land does not enjoy drowning, and we do not enjoy – or to be more specific, our bodies do not enjoy – being given something they are already full on. If we were in tune with our bodies we would recognise the signs they give off when full, stomach ache, bloating and aching.

So we feed into a behaviour pattern of self-abuse, and as we see this does not give us the so called loving relationship with food we think we have. The reality is that we often – very often – beat ourselves up for having fed into this belief of loving food and over-indulging in it. When we eat in this way, we feed into this self-abusing type of behaviour, which we are familiar with. We are not loving food or ourselves. We really do not love the food at all. However, we are somewhat driven by the behaviour it enables, and food is the tool we use to get to this comforting, familiar place. It is not one that we like, but we are used to it – we are used to being in a place we do not like!

In fact, we are very bound by the behaviour food enables, and this is difficult to let go of.

Our comfort zone is to feel guilty that we have just eaten! A good parallel would be to think of every time we go to the pub and have a drink. The smokers will then light up a cigarette because of the association. All of these actions rely on each other and give us a sense of ritual and comfort. As soon as one of these is taken away, we begin to get upset; we feel something is missing, just as when we go to bed we usually wish we had eaten differently and feel guilty about what we have done, and however horrid these feelings are, they are part of the ritual of how we end the day…and we go to sleep with the thoughts of 'I'll be good tomorrow'. I'll have a better day with food tomorrow. What a tall order that is to live up to!

Routine/Habitual Behaviour/Addiction

So what does food do? What sort of behaviour does it enable us to participate in?

Let's look at the following categories to begin this analysis:

What is a routine?

What is an habitual behaviour?

What is an addiction?

For each category list six examples so that you can really identify with them.

Once we have completed the definitions of each of these, we will find that the way we think of an addiction is, in fact, appropriate for habitual behaviour. For example, if we looked at a client attending a 'dry out' establishment for drug or alcohol rehabilitation, we would find that they will often be advised not to return to the environment in which they used to take the drugs, or visit the same old public houses where they used to drink, because by association that environment brings on the old habits – the habitual behaviour.

If we apply this idea of habitual behaviour to food, we see we need to stop believing we are food addicts. We are not. We are caught up, bound into, the behaviour that food enables, and that is self-abuse.

It might be a little uncomfortable to read that we self–abuse, as the immediate examples that come to mind would be of cutting our arms, or causing ourselves pain in a way that we recognise the pain. However, we often feel so full that we have to undo our trousers, and that is pain in a different way. We feel full, but we still eat and sometimes get 'stitches'. This again is over-loading the body. It really is self–abuse. And then there is the weight gain, and this is not kind to us. To carry our extra weight makes life more difficult and a struggle.

Once we are able to admit this, we will be able to empower ourselves to believe in different things and that we have a choice – the choice being that we can change our behaviours. We just need to change our thinking. We need to alter those Euphoric recalls and make sure that the Guardsman and the PA are given the proper file from the Filing Cabinet, the one that informs us that we actually feel angry, remorseful, and guilty, to name but a few feelings we have when we eat inappropriately. The whole 'Treat' analysis could not be further from the truth. In the world of cognitive behavioural therapy, the belief is very much that behaviours can change but only through the change in our thinking. We do need to believe, and I really must emphasis, 'believe': the treat is a treat when we eat a little amount and at the 'right' time.

Real treats do not make us feel horrid!

Answers to the Questions about Routine/Habitual Behaviour/Addiction

A Routine

- Has choice
- An awareness of the self doing it
- Chosen because it is believed to be beneficial in life

- Not problematic if not done sometimes
- Regular

An Habitual Behaviour

- Conditioned
- Sometimes out of awareness
- No choice at all, and with physical implications when withdrawn from
- A driven behaviour
- Usually inherited
- Frequent

An Addiction

This somewhat up for discussion. It appears that the jury is still out on the definition. However, for our purposes we can adopt the definition that an addiction is physiologically driven... and that, more appropriately, an addiction cannot occur unless there is an habitual behaviour in place!

"TO LEARN ABOUT ONESELF IS TO FORGET ONESELF"

"TO FORGET ONESELF IS TO BE ENLIGHTENED BY EVERYTHING"

Chapter Two

EMOTIONAL EATING

In the last chapter we considered the origins of our relationship with food, how our brain works with the thoughts and the memories we have, and consequently how we behave.

In this chapter we will look at the more obvious reasons we overeat and will introduce two types of therapy, Transactional Analysis and Cognitive Behavioural Therapy, which will set a framework upon which we can gain a real understanding.

What Are The Presenting Reasons For Over-Eating?

Due to our euphoric recall, we always think, remember, and believe that food makes us better.

When we become aware of our emotions and feel our emotions, when we are aware of having any feelings at all, we automatically feel uncomfortable, which in turn produces for us a certain sense of vulnerability. Additionally, we feel unsafe, and this is one of the biggest triggers for us to eat.

Many times when we feel an emotion extremely, we feel unsafe with its intensity and often revert to food that dampens down the experience of that discomfort.

It is very much the case that we feed into our emotions, some more than others, the most noticeable ones being:

- Anger

- Stress / Anxiety

- Sadness

- Frustration

- Boredom

- Irritation

- Tiredness

All of these seem to cause a level of discomfort, which in turn takes us away from a familiar place of thinking we are IN CONTROL!

Indeed, if we were to give this list some more time, we would be able to add to it as we become more sensitive to the actual emotions we can feel as human beings.

Another reason for us to eat we shall describe as 'associative'.

To elaborate on this, we would find that we eat because of a connection with something else that we do; we eat through association of something else.

For example, as we discussed in Chapter One, we come home from work and find ourselves standing in the middle of the kitchen, wanting something to eat. Our thoughts are on the fact that we have had a tough day at work and deserve a treat for the day. For as long as we can remember, too, when we come home from being out, either at school or at work, or even if we come in from shopping, or just taking a walk, we will habitually want to eat and or drink.

We have that association of 'coming in from being out', and we have a drink and something to eat.

Let us not forget that most of us have experienced a childhood of coming home from school, and the first thing that our main carers, i.e., mums or dads did for us would be to give us a juice and biscuits…and so the behaviour was learnt.

Other examples for us to be aware of could be:

- When we go out for a drink in the evening with our friends, we usually accompany the occasion with food, so we would go out for a meal and drink. Or as teenagers, we might often find that our night out in the pubs would be finished off with a kebab, or fish and chips, to soak up the alcohol! So drink is associative to food.

- When we settle down in front of the TV of an evening, as a way of unwinding and relaxing, we can often find ourselves becoming bored, both because what we have to watch on TV is not interesting to us and because we find it incredibly difficult to consciously relax. By that, I mean we are either used to living at 200 miles per hour, or being asleep and unconscious in our relaxation. It is not long before we become fidgety and want to do something, and that translates into wanting something to eat, because this both dampens down our uncomfortable feelings of boredom and, actually, eating gives us something to do. So TV is associative to food.

- When we go to the cinema, this evokes the need to eat something, such as popcorn or tubs of ice cream. That was part of the treat of going to the movies when we were children and went with our parents. So cinemas are associated with food – popcorn and tubs of ice cream especially.

And as we begin to think in this way, we begin to tune in to all the other things in life that lead to associative eating.

There is also the simplicity of holding on to certain messages that have been given to us in growing up around food. Let us consider the following thoughts we choose to hold on to:

- **I can see the food and it hasn't cost me anything.** I must make the best of this occasion, as I'm not sure when this situation will come round again. In fact, I'm not sure that it ever will be repeated.

- **Food must not be wasted.** If we go out for a meal, we think we have paid for it, and we do not leave food on the plate for which we have paid. This would be such a waste of money. Even if we are at home and have cooked the meal that we sit down to eat, we still think that we cannot possibly throw food in the bin. We did have to buy it in the first place, and we have put some effort into cooking it. To waste food would be to disrespect the money we earn to buy food, and to disrespect the time, which is very limited, that we spend making the food dish.

- **We must finish the food on our plate.** Otherwise, it will be that 'waste thing' again. We have often been told that there are the starving millions in Africa and how they would do anything to have the very meal we have in front of us. There is also the fact that we would show a lack of appreciation to the person who has cooked it. When we go out to someone's home for a meal, we believe it is very rude not to eat what they provide, because they have taken so much time to make it.

- **It is time to eat.** We believe there are set times to eat, and indeed if we work, we are given the lunchtime slot between 12.00 noon and 2.00 p.m. to have our lunch, so this is very much reinforced by the culture we live and work in. Midday-ish, is lunchtime, 6.00 p.m. is dinnertime, and when we wake up we are told to 'break the fast' and to start the day with a meal.

- **If someone offers food,** then it is only polite to accept it. Food offerings are a sociable thing in our culture, and many a time we believe that when friends come round to see us this is not enough – we are not enough of an offering – so we offer them cakes or biscuits. We bought that packet of biscuits just in case someone came round. Naturally, when we become the visitor, we think we must accept all offerings, because the host has been so kind as to think about us in the first place.

I'm sure you can think of many more circumstances that you feed into. See if you can write others down for yourself.

Keeping in mind the three categories that we have specifically identified for **over-eating,** it would now be useful to go one step further and notice just exactly how` we behave and feel when we eat in these inappropriate moments.

There is a whole different demeanour about us when we eat from a sense of inappropriateness, because we do fundamentally feel uncomfortable when we do this.

So the **way** in which we eat at those times would be:

- Eating quickly

- Eating from the packet / tin / box

- Eating straight out of the fridge

- Eating alone

- Eating in a secret and deceitful way, either by turning our back on others or going into a different room

- Eating sneakily

In other words, we isolate ourselves because we find what we are doing unacceptable to ourselves in the first instance.

So although we were originally feeding into a sense of discomfort, we now exacerbate those feelings by eating in a manner that is really not acceptable to us either and creates yet another set of emotions, such as feeling:

- Naughty

- Ashamed

- Embarrassed

- Depressed

- Angry

- Sad

- Fed up

- Guilty

In addition to this, we also experience the physiological feelings of:

- Bloating

- Sickness

- Lethargy

- Aching

- Heartburn

… Because we have not only eaten quickly to allow the forbidden to happen but also eaten unnecessarily huge amounts. Because we are completely out of tune with what our bodies are telling us, we feel almost compelled, almost driven to fulfil this type of behaviour.

I always think it is useful to become objective at this point and imagine that someone says to us, 'Let's go somewhere to eat that isn't particularly pleasant. Let's stuff food down ourselves so quickly that we are unable to even taste it. We need to make sure that no one else even knows we are doing it, you know. Let's be deceitful about it, no one else can see us, and then we can feel totally horrid, totally guilty, and absolutely crappy about the whole thing.'

Seeing this in the cold light of day, we are able to see how our behaviour really looks. How unkind, even cruel we are to ourselves, and how harshly we treat our bodies. Who wants to let someone do that to themselves? And yet that is exactly what we do!

Ironically, we still believe that we love food.

Not only food in general – because that would not be strictly true – but that food, that particular food…chocolate, crisps, cakes, bread, pasta, cheese, etc., the foods that we eat in the way that has been described in our objective paragraph.

There is also the matter of our identity with food.

We feel the need to identify ourselves around food.

We have strong beliefs that we are a certain type of person in relation to certain foods.

We seem to be able to understand ourselves and the greater world if we can position ourselves somewhere within the food chain, so we give ourselves some sort of title as do our family and friends which results in us calling ourselves 'chocoholics', or 'the Savoury Person', or even 'the Crisp Lover', etc.

This becomes quite precious to us in some way, and we find ourselves being very protective of our 'food identity'. We have almost certainly heard people proclaim, 'I have the sweet tooth and love chocolate', to which others have emphatically answered 'Oh no, crisps are my thing', as if in some bizarre way we are proud of our foible!

The shift we need to make in order to help ourselves is going to involve changing this identity – letting go of some unhelpful identities both in life and around food – and we will need to soul-search to do this.

To let go of our identity around food is no mean feat and can be difficult for us, as sometimes this is the only identity that we think we have.

When it comes to our relationship with food and weight loss, our behaviour pattern is quite clearly defined and in essence easy to understand. For most of our life we have lived through a cycle which has involved either letting go and putting weight on, which is usually the result of us being on our own and being isolated with food, or restricting ourselves, being on a diet, and losing weight. But at least we have, during this time, felt a sense of belonging and camaraderie, as we have become a member of that diet regime or the fat club. Both are extreme behaviours – but consistent with how we approach everything we do in life – and, once again, are how we identify who we are.

If we sit and think, I'm sure we can often recall the many, many times that we have said to ourselves and to others, 'Oh no, I mustn't have that – I am on a diet and I must watch what I eat today,' or "Oh really, I shouldn't, but hey, let's take a day off, and we'll start again tomorrow.'

Both of these examples illustrate how we place ourselves at one end of the spectrum or the other – being very rigid and definite about our restriction, or just letting go and blowing any sense of caution to the wind.

These extremes feed off each other. We will never have one without the other, and both cause us to experience life as a struggle.

Yet, it is the struggle of life that we once again need to identify with. After all, we are the ones that struggle both with food and in life!

This idea – this proposition – might well sound bizarre. Why would we **want** to struggle in life? The idea sounds preposterous, and yet if we think about it, we have always wished we were in that 'better' place, the one everyone else is in, and often we talk of how lucky those thin people are: 'It's not fair! Those thin people can eat what they want, and they never put an ounce on!'

This whole thought places us in a 'bad' and struggling position in the world.

In relation to food, I guess we would respond to this thought that we struggle with it and with weight through no fault of our own; it is just because we naturally love food for the taste and what it delivers to us. Once again, however, that would reinforce the file from the 'filing cabinet' given to the PA, a totally distorted euphoric recall, because when we then swallow the food it all changes.

That peaceful calm and serene moment disappears and is replaced with thoughts of hating ourselves, so in effect the exact opposite, or shall we say extreme, happens, wishing we had not succumbed to the food, and constantly worrying about where that resultant unsightly fat is going to end up, not forgetting the fact that we once again feel ourselves to be a failure.

That first mouthful of our 'picky' food has such a lot to answer for. It gives us that peace, calmness, and serenity in life that we would otherwise not be able to find. Obviously, this food has a head start on delivering these sensations because of our history with it. Additionally, it gives us our 'time out' from the quick and stressful pace of life we lead, and yet it is so short lived.

Let us not forget that we hold extremes around life and food, so when we start to eat our 'picky' foods, we give ourselves permission for this moment to be the 'bad' moment and therefore have to make full use of it. And full use is exactly what we do make of it: we eat enough for, let's say, two days.

There is also the conflict of not really knowing where else, or how else, to get that same sense of relief from life and feel so calm and at peace with ourselves. We can do nothing but look in the same place for more of the experience. Unfortunately, what actually occurs is that with the ever-increasing quantity that is eaten, the sense of relief and calm subsides and is taken over by anger and frustration as well as guilt and shame.

So we need to get to the bottom of this cycle. On the one hand, we think the food is wonderful and indeed have a certain identity around specific types.

Our euphoric recall, you know the distorted memory, will have us think nothing other than wonderful things around food. Yet the reality is that in the here and now we have distorted the origins of the behaviour around our 'picky' foods so that we now eat to feel like rubbish.

If we take a step back from this cycle of extremes, we can ask ourselves: 'Why is this sensory fulfilment so absolutely important to us that we repeatedly go down the same route to find the rainbow and think that this time it will be different and we shall touch it and feel such a sense of relief from the struggle of life?'

It is as if we need to hit our head on the brick wall time and time again, because we so need that 'moment out' of this struggle of life. We also need to have a sensory sense of self – and boy, that first mouthful of food, or in this example, the knock of the head on the wall, does that for us, as well providing a sense of existence and identity for us.

Is it because all the other times of the day, every day, we concentrate on other people and their needs and wants, placing them even before our own, so that our own self-presence dwindles to a level of insignificance.

We give out and do so much for others that the only way we know how to give to ourselves is through food.

So What Are The Behaviours That Food Enables?

What is our behaviour pattern with food both from a small aspect and then the larger one?

- We eat so quickly that we do not even taste the food.

- We eat alone, when others are out of the room or away.

- We eat out of draws, cupboards and fridges as well as tins, packets and boxes…

- We eat copious quantities in a very focussed and self-indulgent way.

In short, and yet with the importance given by 'the higher echelons', we need to realise that we eat without giving ourselves self-respect and value, and in return merely offer the same to the food that we eat.

If we were to enjoy food, and also respect and value it, we would emulate the behaviours of people such as Jamie Oliver and Gordon Ramsey, who have such passion, interest, and respect for it, along with desire and an almost seductive relationship with it.

They are wholly in love with the goodness of food, all food.

We find we are a million miles from where they stand and see that our behaviours just enable us to self-harm and self-destruct.

We are not being kind to ourselves at all when eating the way that we do. I do think it is important to realise that putting on lots of weight, lots of fat, is in itself self–harming.

When we consider the health issues associated with weight gain, the self-harm can be quite radical and not dissimilar to people who self-harm with a razor blade, cutting their arms. The only reason we get away with it and do not receive the same amount of or type of judgement, is because we use a socially acceptable medium, namely food – acceptable because, is food not essential to survival?

How do we know that food enables in us such behaviours – the behaviour of self-harm and self-destruction? Because once we have chewed, and swallowed food we again feel:

- Naughty

- Ashamed

- Embarrassed

- Depressed

- Angry

- Guilty…

… As well as

- Sick

- Lethargic

- Aching

- Bloated

This is not a great way to feel. It is none other than self-destructive and self-harming. So let's really analyse this and take this notion deep into ourselves.

To Self-Harm

We have over-ridden the body's messages of being full (the message given by the hypothalamus to the Guardsman) and allowed our 'head' to rule us with all the thoughts we have – the expectations, all the excuses that we hold as valid and reasonable.

We have eaten to the point that we have gained weight, consequently putting ourselves at a higher risk of experiencing health problems. We have put our bodies under a huge strain and our mental state into a very lonely place, because when we gain weight we just want to isolate ourselves and hide away.

Does this sound harsh to us? Is our immediate response to deny the very truth of the situation we place ourselves in? Yet to realise this will empower us.

This is not about more of the same, and thinking that we have done everything wrong, and that we are useless. Stop there if you are making that judgement call!

Awareness empowers, and empowerment enables us to move on. The realisation of what we have read so far will empower us to see the truth of our position amidst this chaos of weight, food, and ourselves. By understanding totally why we use food, we then have choice. By realising what our fat means to us, we then have choice.

To help us understand the message

'Food Enables Behaviour'

Let us look at the work of a man called Eric Berne, who has given us a therapy called Transactional Analysis.

He states that we have within us three different sides, called 'ego states'. We react to others and to situations from one of these ego states, depending on how that other person affects us. To be more specific, we have the Parent ego, Adult ego, and Child ego. The ego that we feed into is almost always the Child ego state, the six year old. After all, it is a child that has the need to be:

- Secretive

- Naughty

- Deceitful

- Wanting to 'get away with it'.

… And will use food for those behaviours.

I worked with a lady a couple of years ago, and on one occasion she came to me with fear all over her face. When I asked her if she was OK, she proceeded to tell me she had eaten three Cadbury Cream Eggs, from a pack of three. More specifically, she was aware that she had eaten them so quickly she hadn't really either tasted them or enjoyed them. More to the point, whilst she was just nearing the end of her third egg, she had heard her husband coming down the stairs, and in a complete panic she hastily gathered all the wrappers and packaging in her hand, proceeded to roll up the top of her sleeve, and with her arm, pushed her hand to the bottom of the kitchen bin so that her husband would not find out what she had just done.

'Did you enjoy the eggs and then hiding the evidence?' I asked her. And she looked at me, then laughed and said, 'It was fun and exciting. I felt very naughty and like a little girl. It was pretty good to get away with it!'

It is the child in us that eats copious quantities of 'picky' foods, that eats quickly without tasting them, or even avoids putting them on a plate and giving ourselves time to enjoy it. It is the child in us that needs immediate gratification, which is why diets have always had their part to play in this. A little girl or boy has no sense of long-term outcomes in life. There is only the sense that right now, right in this moment, counts. When we see food it enables us to fulfil this immediacy, this belief that 'now'' is the only time that matters, which in turn enables us the behaviour to eat whatever we see.

Within these three ego states – Parent, Adult and Child – there are two ego states that have what are called 'sub egos', so within each Parent and Child there are particular aspects to be aware of. For us, it is important to know about the Critical Parent and the Nurturing Parent.

Taking this one step at a time, let us look at what we mean by the Critical Parent.

A very good exercise for us to do that enables us to clearly understand the Critical Parent is for us to make a list of all the 'I shoulds' that we hold on to in our lives, that we try to live up to, and believe we must aspire to. So to start off, here are a few examples:

- I should…clean the house every week,

- I should…get up earlier,

- I should…cook every day for my family,

- I should… see my mum every day,

- I should….always be polite,

Once we get into the swing of this, we find that we have many 'I shoulds'.

Now, with the same list change 'I should' **to 'If I really wanted to, I could…'**

When you have completed rewriting your list with the 'If I really wanted to, I could' read each list out aloud. What do you notice?

It feels very different to talk of what we want to do as opposed to what we think we should do. You might sense a different tone, energy, speed, and emotion with each list. For instance, the 'should' list might possibly hear us methodically drone on, because a lot of the listed 'shoulds' sound so boring, so same-same, and so distant from us, where as the 'If I really wanted to, I could' is more bouncy and tunes us into ourselves more. We feel less told to do things and more in command of whether we actually really want to do whatever it is we write down. In conclusion, there is choice!

If we really tuned in to ourselves, we would find that the 'I Should' list produces feelings of anger as well as feelings of guilt, because whatever we do on this list, there is always more to do. Life is such a chore. We never get to that calm place of having done it all, never achieve the whole list, so the list initiates and perpetuates feelings of sadness, guilt, anger, and, in general, discomfort, along with the thoughts of never being able to 'do' enough.

Let us analyse where the 'shoulds' come from. 'Should' comes from an external source:

- Society states we 'should'

- Parents state we 'should'

- Everyone else states we 'should'

And we believe in them, and take them on, because we automatically believe in others more than we believe in ourselves. We do at some level think others are 'right', and we listen to them.

Yet when another person tells us we 'should' do this or that, what they are really saying is that they believe – from where they are standing and being the person that they are – that the 'should' is a good idea. The tragedy here is that the other person is projecting, if not quite wilfully forcing their beliefs onto another, i.e., us, and if we are not careful we forget that we have our own way of doing things, our own way of living. We can see this clearly with the diet system. We have gone to these regimes and taken on their Critical Parent position, because they tell us what we should do to lose weight, they tell us what foods to eat, and they tell us how to eat them. However, for the most part, we know what to eat, but we need to understand why we don't eat it when left to our own devices.

So although we strive to follow these 'shoulds', because they originate from an external someone, they rarely fit exactly into our own style of being who we are.

(We need to mention that there are extreme cases of 'shoulds' that the majority need to follow: we should keep away from fire; we should not stand in the middle of the road, etc. However, we can easily turn these into a 'want', because we do not want to get burnt or run over, we do not want to do these things because we are aware of not wanting the outcome)

There is conflict around this 'should' list, and we can very often find ourselves not doing the thing that we believe we should because, the 'six-year-old child' in us wants to rebel and be against the whole 'should' system.

On the other hand, we strive hard to do what we 'should', as we want to be seen as the 'good girl', and we are caught up in believing that what we do provides us with a level of 'goodness', but the list never finishes, and we never do that thing well enough, so we keep ourselves in the powerless, place of always thinking that we 'should be doing more', we 'should be doing better'.

So the Critical Parent talks with the prefixes of:

- 'Should'

- 'Must'

- 'Have To'

- 'Got To

- 'Need To`

Now that you are aware of this, go out and live your day. See how often you and others use these words, and see how you and others respond.

The response to the Critical Parent is always going to be from the Child ego state. However, we have two sub-ego states within that child, and they are the Adaptive Child and the Rebellious Child.

Whether we react from the adaptive or rebellious` Child towards the Critical Parent depends on how we feel, but for the most part we fulfil, as much as we can, the Adaptive Child's duties. Whatever happens, we either follow the 'should', or we think 'to hell with it' and rebel.

The tension between these two child ego states - tension that we hold in ourselves – is the 'driving force that starts the eating. Also, it is the Rebellious Child that will go out on their own and feed out of packets. The objective example I spoke of earlier asked why would we want to be so unkind to ourselves. Here is the answer: the Rebellious Child will often cut off her nose to spite her face. This is our 'opt out clause', but with a little or sometimes a lot of anger because for the rest of the time we are pleasing people.

The 'If I Really Wanted to, I Could' statement originates in the Adult ego state. This we know because it is a respectful statement, and adults respect choice. It feels kinder to us, don't you think? We can feel more relaxed because we are able to tune into the choice that this offers. We feel we can own this list. We can start to make decisions and feel more positive about ourselves. The list can become ours: what do we want and what shall we choose to do that will benefit ourselves?

In order that we might fully empower ourselves with this exercise, we can look down our list and cross out all the things we do not want to do. However, let us focus on the 'want', and take this word into consideration in a larger sense.

We might think that we do not want to do the ironing ever again. Who loves ironing? To get up on time rather than squeeze a few minutes more in bed – who wants to do that? And then there is the house cleaning. Good god, who on earth wants to do that? Let's be real about this!

Yet, at the same time, we will probably want to wear ironed clothes and look smart. Putting on that newly ironed shirt makes us feel really good about ourselves.

Getting to work at a more leisurely pace, and feeling calmer and more relaxed because we have had a coffee sitting down in our kitchen, as well as looking so much better because we have had time to put ourselves together, could easily be a huge want for us.

Then there is the 'clean house thing'. Do we want our home environment to be chaotic, or to be 'clean-ish' and orderly? Can we relax more if it is the latter? Almost, quite possibly. So I guess we might want to do the thing that produces those results. Otherwise, we sit with a lot of irritation, it bugs us and we use the not doing it against ourselves, in truth we do not feel comfortable when we do not do these things and that is not what we want.

This is about realising what we as individuals want, realising our own personal standards of life and how we want things done and things to look. We do these things because we want them done for ourselves, as opposed to, from external pressures and for other people. One of the noticeable changes that we often make is that we take ownership of our own needs and our own timeframe; we do it when we want to and because we want to, In other words, when that particular thing begins to irritate us, we know it is the right time for us to do it.

To understand the real depth of a want, it becomes necessary to look at the bigger picture of our lives and decide if the outcome of various jobs is what we want. We need to accept that we want to do the job for the outcome.

Going back to our list, then, let us cross all the things out that we do not want to do and leave the 'stuff' we do want to do. We need to then ask ourselves why do we not do them?

If we immediately find that we start to answer this question with,

'There is not enough time,'
'I am too tired,'
'There are too many other things to do'

.... Then maybe it is the case that we do not want to do these things enough, because if we really want to do them enough, then we will find the time, have the energy, and prioritise. Again, there is always the case of the Critical Parent telling us, 'We are only allowed to do the things we want to do when everything that we should do has been done.' Unfortunately, this message keeps us away from our wants, because, as I have said before, the 'should list' is phenomenal and takes all of our time.

So let's look carefully, and let go of the 'shoulds', and see what we really want to do, and think about why we do not then do it! Apart from the Critical Parent, we must search for reasons why we do not do what we want.

Maybe on your list you are still caught up with thinking that you want to do the 'should' things, so think really hard about the wants, and when you are left with a list of real wants, go out and do them. Truly let go of the 'shoulds', and feed yourself differently – not with food but with things that can 'give back' to you in a more beneficial way.

Many of us talk about the devil on our left shoulder and the angel on our right. If we apply this to Eric Berne's theory of Transactional Analysis, the Critical Parent would be our devil and the Nurturing Parent the angel.

The Nurturing Parent is the side of us that is more sympathetic, is kinder to us, and far less judgemental. The type of messages our Nurturing Parent would gives us are:

- 'If you are feeling, tired have a rest and do whatever it is later.'

- 'You have done enough for today, go and have some fun.'

- 'Don't worry, everything will turn out OK.'"

As we can clearly see, and very quickly, these messages are not the ones we hear a lot.

Let us now look at the diagram of the way Eric Berne's theory works:

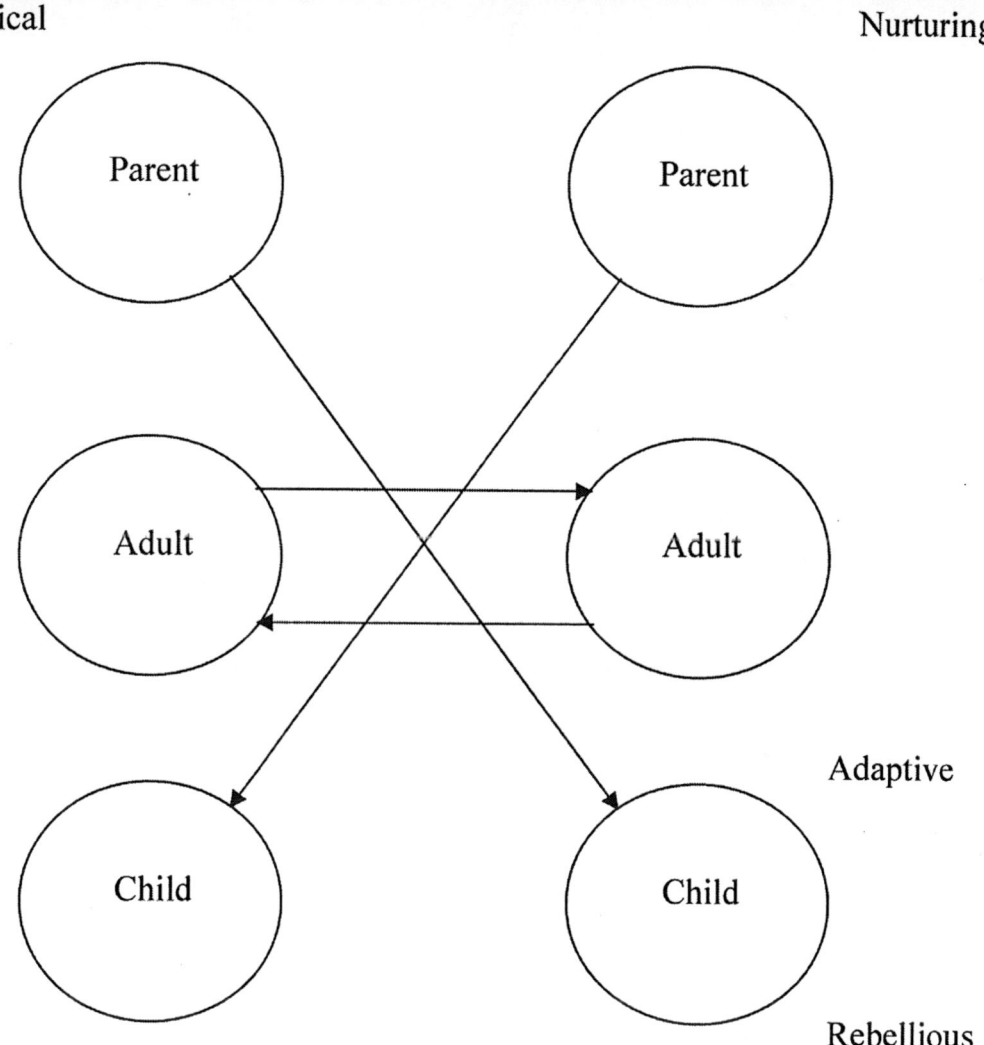

Another sub-ego state we have is the Free Child, and this side of us responds to the Nurturing Adult because, as we are given permission to be kind to ourselves, we allow ourselves to be responsive to how we feel both on an emotional level as well as on a physical level.

Most of us believe that if we allow this to truly evolve, then most of us will do nothing. This is so not the case because most of us do not want to do 'nothing' all the time!

There has to be a lot of trust in this type of relationship. Unfortunately, many of us have long lost the art of true trust, because our Critical Parent has very little trust, and we have a lot of that parent in us.

As we can now understand from the diagram, we react to the Critical Parent in one of two ways. For the most part, we act from our Adaptive Child, working hard to please the Critical Parent, always doing what we believe we `should` for others and helping others.

Possibly a little more context needs to be added at this point. The Critical Parent is not only a side of ourselves; it is also seen in, and heard from, other people. So for many of us, it is other people that we see as being the Critical Parent, and we most definitely impose this Critical Parent on our close relationships. Not only do we have the internal tussle between our own ego states, we also have the burden of other people involuntarily adding to this conflict. The word 'involuntarily' must be added here, as often we go around in life not having a clue that others have imposed on us all manner of beliefs.

So where do we place ourselves in this diagram? Well, the strongest argument we involve ourselves in is the red-lined relationship, that of Critical Parent and Adaptive Child. We are so extremely Adaptive in our lives, and are driven to focus on other peoples needs so much, that we have to opt out somehow, someway. We have to have a behaviour, or a time, or a way, in which we tell ourselves to say to everyone and everything else, 'Go away and leave me alone', and this comes from the Rebellious Child, the six-year-old that, if you remember, we feed into! The food is the tool that we use to do all of these things, and that enables the behaviour.

We want to have a tantrum. At the point we choose to have one, we have absolutely had enough of life and doing all of these things for other people, and we want to punish every one and have a real go at them all.

However, we ultimately have a go at ourselves, and we use food to do this, which would bring to fruition the behaviour of self-harming.

At the same time, our need is to opt out of the pressure and the stress we feel in this moment, so we go for the 'time out' scenario as well.

The behaviour becomes two–fold, if not multi-facetted. However, it all amounts to the same needs being fulfilled.

We are secretive and have fun eating a chocolate bar when no one else is looking. We get some excitement by being deceitful and hiding the wrappers. We use only our fingers with this food, as to use a knife and fork would bring the eating into the proper place. We are able to forget the stresses and strains of life in this eating moment, so the Rebellious Child is also very useful.

In Conclusion

Let us now see how this theory works with all of these different ego states.

If we talk to ourselves from the Critical Parent place – or indeed, if others talk to us from that same ego state, then the word 'should' will be used. In response to that, we will either be the Adaptive Child, and follow through with that 'should', or we will be the Rebellious Child, and not only not do the 'should' but in addition to this behave in a very tantrum-like way, and add to the not doing. Hence we probably eat a bar of chocolate, or a packet of crisps, thus feeding into the guilt we have of not doing the 'should'.

If we let go, even only a little, of the Critical Parent and balance her out with some Nurturing Parent, we would bring balance into our lives.
This would manifest in a way that would find us doing more of what we want. The impact of this is seen in how we go to the food less often for that metaphorical hug, because we find that we do not need it so much, as we are hugging ourselves more frequently in the way that we are being kind to ourselves.

It must be emphasised that we are not getting rid of the Critical Parent totally, as she does have her own importance and use. After all, we have to keep our distance from fire, or we will not stay safe, so we are able to see the use of the Critical Parent in various situations.

We must be quite clear that we know that we will always have every ego state within us, and that we work from each and every one of them. It is right to do so, but in a balanced way:

- We need all of them; they do serve us well when in balance.

- Too much Rebellious Child finds us 'cutting our nose to spite our face'.

- Too much Adaptive Child finds us not tending to our own needs.

- When the Critical Parent is the only pervading ego state, we are driven to be extreme in our rebellious behaviour, and hence we gorge on our 'picky' foods.

The idea is not to get rid of these ego states – this would be impossible – but to keep them in balance.

So What is Food to Us?

We now begin to see a pattern emerge, and food starts to show up as a mechanism, a tool that enables a certain behaviour from a certain ego state.

We use food to rebel, from that Rebellious Child place. We need the Rebellious Child, as our lives are otherwise so 'responsible' and even seen as 'mundane'. It is fun, therefore, to be secretive and deceitful, and, as we know, food is the ideal tool for behaving in this way. Yet the long-term outcome of this immediate fun is that we are kept from liking ourselves, as we self-harm and put weight on.

The belief is that we 'love' food, and yet food is only truly loved when it is not being used to destroy ourselves.

As children, we were often limited to the foods available, and 'picky' foods were definitely limited. As children, if we are told 'NO' around anything, we want it even more. As we have learnt, we feed into the six-year-old child.

In our later years, I guess, we are still reacting to that 'NO', and if we search deep within ourselves we might realise this is still the case.

I know for myself that in my early years I was given the message that an apple was a fruit best eaten; today I still baulk at eating one, and yet when I breach that resistance, I very much enjoy an apple.

"WE ARE ONLY WILLING
TO LIVE IF
WE ARE
WILLING TO LEARN!"

"THE KEY TO GOOD
HEALTH IS
MODERATION IN ALL
THINGS, BOTH
PHYSICALLY AND
EMOTIONALLY!"

Chapter Three

WHAT DOES BEING FAT REALLY MEAN TO US?

We Choose to Get Fat

'What a perfectly crazy notion', I hear you say, and yet if we can fully accept this, and all that this statement suggests, then we can empower ourselves to make the choice to let go of the fat and to find a size at which we are happy.

We feel out of control around food:

- We think that food is our enemy

- We think that we are addicted to food.

- We think that life isn't fair and that we are a victim of life.

If we stop all of these negative thoughts – that in truth only support us in believing that we are a victim – and find different thoughts that benefit us, we will see a change in our behaviour and ultimately find answers that give:

- Choice,

- Empowerment,

… And ultimately a happiness that we have not experienced for the best part of our lives.

To explain 'choosing to become fat', we need to look into our subconscious so that we can understand the core of our belief system.

So what use does fat have that we might choose to be fat? We look at ourselves carrying all of this unwanted fat, and we hate it and are repulsed by it.

We can barely look at ourselves below our necks, because all we can see are the hideous lumps and bumps, and trying to dress ourselves when we're fat is so difficult; we never look how we want to… and then we read that

… we choose this!

It must feel as though the world has gone mad, and yet once again, we must read that, yes, we do choose to get fat.

No one else puts the food in our mouths. Let's work on the premise that there is no hereditary reason for our size, no genetic disposition, and that the fact is simple: We have to balance the amount of food we eat – and consequently put into our bodies – with the amount of energy we use up; otherwise we will gain weight!

Nothing else need come into the equation, and as I write this, I can sense many of you thinking, 'Oh, but what about… this, and what about …that', and 'I know people who can eat as much as they like and still never put a pound on.'

This would be coming from the 'victim' inside us.

The 'victim' sense is something we shall look at later, but for now I'm sure we understand the meaning of victim, how victims suffer and struggle with everything in life and basically feel 'hard done by'!

So as victims we try to find external reasons for our distress, thinking this excuses us from solving the problem, and yet in reality all that we do is give away our power; we relinquish any belief of having any choice around whatever problem we have, which renders us incapable, and this is exactly how we feel when it comes to our weight and food.

50

What we are probably not aware of is that our size and our fat is quite a fundamental part of us; it is a part of who we are and how we identify ourselves (this we have already talked about when it comes to food, and now we must register this identity issue around our size).

Other people also identify us with our size in mind. How often have we heard other people say to us when we have been on a diet and lost weight, 'Oh no, you mustn't lose anymore weight – you'll be thinner than me', or 'You have always been the larger daughter in the family'.

We live in society being the weight that we are, or having a struggle with our weight and it is our familiar place. Why else do we think we have lost the weight only to put it all back on and some more… because however great it feels to be thin we, are not used to it, not comfortable with it and all that being thin brings with it and are therefore not able to fully enjoy it.

To enjoy our lives is also outside of our usual 'victim' place too; we are used to struggling, so we return to our familiar place by putting the weight back on.

We have found a use for our fat, and that is why we choose to keep it.

So how does the fat help us, and what does the fat signify to us?

- That we are able to downplay ourselves because of our size. We can joke about ourselves (even if it is very damaging for us). We become used to enabling people to laugh at us because of our size, our fat. This becomes self-ridicule and falls into the pattern of self-harm and abuse that we have already touched on in previous chapters, and this is truly really sad for us. However, we do have a talking point that can save us from any awkward silences: this self-humiliation can break the ice and make friends quickly…. and we feel comfortable about this.

- That we are able to be other peoples friends without being a threat. There are many people who can only have 'a fat friend' because only then are they able to feel good about themselves and feel safe and secure. When it comes to boyfriends of our girlfriends, we can laugh and have fun with them; we can even flirt slightly with them, because under pinning all of this is the belief that no one would fancy a fat girl. So it enables us to make loads of friends, not only with girls, but with boys too, because we are seen as 'not serious'. Once again, however, this places us in the position of lower ranking and of being the victim.

- That we are usually not considered for energetic activities, as others are too embarrassed to ask us to join in. In fact, we are rarely asked to participate in things, as other people feel uncomfortable asking us fat people to do so, just in case we are physically unable. So being fat ultimately gets us out of saying no, which is quite an uncomfortable word to say. Thus immediately the fat gives us an 'opt out' clause, without our having to cause any awkwardness for anyone.

- That we can be comfortable in our clothes. The type of clothes made for fat people usually allow for growth, so they have elastic waistbands and are made from stretchy material. Due to the discomfort we feel about our bodies, physically these clothes are a kindness to us, as we really do not like to be reminded of how we look by tight restricting clothes. This would seem like a knife in the back.
We are trying hard to disconnect from our physicality. As soon as we lose the fat, we feel a greater sense of restriction, and we find that the clothes reflect this by being styled with rigid waistbands and in materials such as cotton and linen – in other words, non-giving materials, which in turn causes us to believe that we must be constantly vigilant with ourselves... and that really does

seem like hard work, and very boring. The argument is, therefore, that we can 'slob' and be comfortable when we are large, and, more to the point, eat whatever we like, which takes very little effort!

- That we can be left alone; Often people appear to keep their distance, because they can feel uncomfortable with our size. The reality for us is that we often think that people do not say hello or talk to us when they could, because to ourselves we think the fat excludes us. We are able to think, 'It's because I'm fat that this happened'. So fat keeps us apart from people which in turn keeps us safe, and we think `safe` because only too often in our past have we been let down and hurt by others, especially when we have allowed ourselves to become close to them.

In some way this last reason can very much be seen as the real issue around fat. We have experienced varying degrees of pain and almost always because of other people, and/or the circumstances of life, so we believe it is safer to keep away from them and hide behind our fat. And as we find it difficult to say `No' and speak up for ourselves, this works well.

Letting people get close to us can potentially cause us pain.

Once again, here is another fun but very telling exercise for us to complete.

Let us begin to understand how our subconscious is working, both against us and for us. Finishing the following sentences, with very little thought; do not censor your immediate response, and see what you write:

If I ate whatever I wanted, I would.......................................
If I were as thin as I wanted, I could not ....

Being thin means that I would.......................................

Men would...

Women would..

Fat women are...

Fat men are...

Now lets look at how you might have completed the sentences and what that will mean to us:

If I ate whatever I wanted, I would.... become bigger than ever and probably explode – in other words, get really fat.

Immediately we see that you do not believe in yourself.

Why do you want to explode? Oh, you don't? So why do you want to eat the food that will make you explode?

You reply that you do not want to eat the food that makes you fat...and so we need to ask why would you do something that gives you the outcome you do not desire and where else in life do you engage in doing something when you do not want the outcome?

We have to look at the word 'want'. If you do not want to get fat, then do not eat the food that makes you fat. Don't forget that you can have all the foods but not the large quantities and know that you must just find a balance.

Think of the Critical Parent at this point, the six-year-old girl who does not focus on the long term but just on the short term. It almost becomes a competition between the short-term immediate gratification and the long-term accountability. We must not forget, too, that the Critical Parent is always telling us what to eat so as soon as we talk of 'want', we move into retaliating and the Rebellious Child and start to 'Eat for England'.

The freedom felt in 'Just eat whatever you want, with no external restrictions imposed on you' implies letting go, so we move out of the Adaptive Child place and into the Rebellious one. Hence we believe we feed for England, etc. After all, if no one is telling you what to eat, then of course you will 'go mad'. Who would want to be sensible? And this is merely reactionary, from the six-year-old's perspective.

So you have finished the sentence from your subconscious, which is important to recognise. The sentence is not wrong, but it does illustrate the very thought that is fundamentally the damaging one. You truly believe that if left to your own devices you will eat `for England`.

If we take into account the philosophy of Cognitive Behavioural Therapy, we will embrace the fact that our behaviour is in direct relation to our thinking. Just look at how your subconscious works against you: not believing in yourself, and thinking that food has the upper hand, and you have no choice. If you do not want to get fat, then I wonder why you would do something to give an outcome you do not want!

If I were as thin as I wanted, I could not... eat what I wanted and have all of those 'nice' things that I so enjoy.

This is where we begin to realise that we think being thin is really restricting, and quite boring; we can't eat the crisps, chocolate, cream cakes, and all those '' foods, and they are our treats.

We think we can only eat the 'rabbit food' when we are thin. Additionally, there is the complication of believing we have to be part of all that frenetic living and have to join in with everything, because others will ask more of us and want to include us more. As we find the word 'no' so difficult to say, this will cause us huge problems; so it's hardly surprising that we do not want to be thin.

Being thin means that:

I would… be so happy. Able to buy clothes I actually like, rather than only the clothes that fit me. Being able to go into any shop and know I could find something to fit in amongst the normal sizes. I would be able to look great and join in with the fun of life, because I would be more agile. And I wouldn't have to work so hard at looking good, as it would come far more naturally with my thinner body – all those lumps and bumps will have gone, and all the effort to conceal them would not have to be made. Such freedom and joy!

So now we see how loosing the weight would bring so much joy to us, make us free and able, and for the first time in a long time we can begin to truly live.

This is our inspiration, this is our focus, and this is us thinking outside the 'victim' place.

Men would… find me attractive, look at me more, and actually take me seriously, rather than see me as the fat person who has no sexuality. They would hold the door open for me and flirt with me.

Although this, on the one hand, sounds great and everything we have longed for, on the other, it can also feel scary, and we can feel quite vulnerable around the new-found command coming from being sexual beings. We have hidden ourselves away for some time behind our fat. The way we dress when we are fat is to cover ourselves up; we wear dark colours. As mentioned before, the only style of clothes we can buy is stretchy and baggy – there is no 'angle' or clean-cut definition to them.

So when we lose our weight we change our appearance, rightly so, and are happy to show off the contours of our body more. We feel happy, so our colours become more interesting and lighter too. (If this change is not made, then it is almost certain that the weight will return, because there will have been no reason for losing it. We will not have tuned into our sense of pride at looking better, and we will feed ourselves back into our fat clothes).

This change in our appearance will, without doubt, bring us some un-asked for attention, which although sounding great, can also bring on feelings of guilt if we are already in a relationship. There can be a sense of betrayal, because the trust that has been invested in our relationship by our partner will seemingly have been compromised by other men desiring us too, and all because we are wearing more 'hugging' type clothing and walking with a spring in our step. Is this right?' we ask ourselves. 'Are we being faithful?' It can certainly feel uncomfortable.

Equally, we might be in a relationship that is unsatisfactory to us, that we are not happy in, but which we have tolerated because of our weight and our beliefs that we deserve no better, nor indeed could do any better.

So if we look at losing weight and how the dynamics alter when it comes to the opposite sex, we can understand how fat keeps us safe, and keeps us away from all this confusion.

Women would… be more competitive, be 'bitchy' to me, and not like me.

When we think about us larger women, there is camaraderie. We believe that we all understand each other's 'unfortunate' position in society. There is a sense of being 'victims' together, all helping each other and being supportive to each other.

When we look outside of our Fat Women's Group, we often feel a tension and competitiveness, especially between thin women, around how to look. Coming out of the 'fat club'— where we think that like-minded and similarly placed women are empathic and kind to each other — automatically puts us in amongst women in the 'harsh club', and we can see it as cold, as callous and serious.

Yet again our sub-conscious works against us: why would we want to place ourselves into that cold environment and out of this cuddly, cosy group? Being fat keeps us cushioned from harshness!

Fat women are... sad, unhappy, lazy, out of control (and any other derogatory judgement).

All this serves to tell us is that we project onto others that which on some level we think of ourselves.

Whilst we remain fat, we fight with ourselves. Our belief that we are all of the aforementioned things is why we drive ourselves to 'do' so much, and tire ourselves out.

This fits in very much with the work that comes later.

Thin women are... happy, sexy, able to look good all the time, serious, sad, bitchy, and competitive.

All of these traits once again reflect to us our own judgements that we make about thin women, and prove to us why indeed we have not become thin before, or indeed stayed thin for longer. Thin is far too stressful and 'open'; there is nothing to keep us buffered from the horrid things in life!

The Conclusion

We really begin to see that although on a conscious, cognitive level (thinking level) we quite naturally want to lose our fat, we have a sub-conscious that sabotages us. Some of the reasons might be surprising for us to read and acknowledge, yet they have not been given to us by another; these are the thoughts that we hold on to at a deeper level. These thoughts show how we **feel** about fat and thin, and they play a huge part in us keeping fat.

For as long as we are fat, we can be safe and almost hide away from life and from people. We can also be a member of the 'fat women's club', which is kinder, more empathic, and understanding. The club puts us outside normal society, and therefore grants us special attention, which is very important to us. Without this attention, albeit negative a lot of the time, we have a belief that we will fade into the background in a way that would be devastating.

For as long as we are fat, we can obsess about being on a diet, we can obsess about our weight and our appearance, and we can obsess about wanting something that we believe we can never have: to be thin and happy.

We can always have the struggle of life, and we can be that victim.

We also have something to do – we always have the task of needing to lose weight. When we take hold of those moments in our lives, when we allow ourselves to let go of the fat, we can gain some `kindly` attention from others, and then we can have glimpses of feeling good about ourselves. Unfortunately, this is not a place we are comfortable in, and so we unconsciously take ourselves back into the old 'victim' place.

So being fat enables… quite an irony, quite a mix of things, which is why so many of us are confused by the whole subject!

Being fat really does allow us some 'difference'. We are outside the norm of society, and we like that because it affords us some special consideration, although we are not consciously aware of this.

Being thin, on the other hand, will mean that we have to say 'yes' to everything. Others will invite us into the fold more and want to engage in our company more. We will have no excuse not to join in with physical activities, no excuse to keep us at home and away from socialising. With the additional inability to say 'no', we can almost see how being thin is far too scary a place to be in.

Also, we look normal and therefore warrant no extra attention.

We believe we would have to eat healthily forever and would never able to indulge in the 'nice' foods of life. We would have to be in control all the time, 'restricting' ourselves, constantly being 'sensible', in short, eat 'rabbit food' – now that sounds like a real 'wow' place to be in. It is not surprising we do not want to stay thin for long.

Being in the normal place doesn't offer us any goal to strive for; it seems as though there is nothing to achieve; in fact, if we carried on, I think we would begin to find this place quite boring.

We realise that being in the 'fat place' and the 'thin place' has lots of contradictions; our emotions are not always in tune with our thoughts, and therefore it is hardly surprising that we have not succeeded in losing our weight, or indeed if we have, that we have not kept the weight off.

Let us summarise what the different aspects are:

Being Fat

- Comes between us and other people, which keeps us from being hurt.

- Enables us to hate ourselves – which although it sounds awful– is the long-established and familiar relationship we have with ourselves, so it is comfortable.

- Gives us a valid excuse to opt out, and when we find it almost impossible to say the word no, this is very useful to us.

- Brings us attention. When we are fat, we attend to ourselves significantly more than when we are not. We obsess about our weight and bring that obsession into our relationships, too.

Being Thin

- Brings on the belief that we have to do everything, because we are now physically able to do so. This is somewhat overwhelming to us and can cause us some anxiety.

- Allows us to like ourselves, which is a very new and different relationship to have with ourselves, so it is unfamiliar territory for us.

- Gives us attention that we might not ask for or want, so we can feel very much out of control, and that once again is not comfortable.

- Creates a sense of vulnerability, almost opens us to the world, which can cause anxieties.

- Means we are normal, and this is definitely odd for us.

When We Are Thin

We constantly dream that being thin will give us so much happiness! 'Thin' means a certain freedom from struggle, in life and most definitely with our weight. Not having to work so hard at looking good because we can just dress in anything, and we'll be able to look good because thin works.

Our confidence increases; we feel great about ourselves; and our increased self-worth shows as we walk tall and, integrate into the social side of life.

We feel great about our appearance, and can for the first time connect our head to our body, and realise we are one whole being, and not be disgusted by ourselves. We can treat ourselves with kindness and love, instead of abuse.

Being thin means our dream has been achieved, and now we are one of those lucky thin people instead of being one of the 'victim' fat people.

Life couldn't be any better!

So why don't we stay thin when we get thin?

Answer

The useful excuse for everything negative that happens to us... is gone!

We now think we must turn ourselves into 'rabbits', eating only lettuce and tomatoes, with a bit of chicken and fish.

We say yes to everything and everyone, because we cannot say no, and now a lot of people start to ask us to join in with so much, because we look so able. Consequently we become very busy... very busy...too busy. Of course, the simple solution would be to say no, but we think that people will dislike us if we say that, so we feel stuck with doing everything, and anyway we do like to join in with life.

We feel energised by this different identity and conflicted by thinking that this is the place we have longed to be in, but we still feel something is missing. We do not have the struggle with our weight. That is missing... at long last... and yet still this thin place is not what we had envisaged it to be; it is not the utopia we had dreamed of.

Let us slow down the process of reaching the weight goal and analyse what happens to us from the moment we are in that long-awaited thin, or thinner, place.

We wake up on 'that' morning, and the relief of not having to 'do that diet' any more, because we have reached our goal, is huge. Other people have been giving us compliments for a while now; we have been receiving lots of positive attention, and this produces a huge 'feel good factor' for us.

However, it is only the change itself that causes others to make comments; as time passes, we will not have changed our size, as we are now working desperately at staying the same weight.

So we are now no different; we are 'normal'. No one comments on how good we look, and no one is interested in our weight loss. The honeymoon has ended.

Our increase in self-worth and self-confidence is very much tied up with the achievement of our weight loss and the compliments driven by that weight loss. Unfortunately, when that achievement becomes an old one, the messages that surround it become forgotten, and we see ourselves sliding back into the old familiar place with the old familiar thinking patterns: 'Well, I think I've done well today, but no one else seems to have noticed so I'll give myself a treat.' We all know what type of treat we give ourselves... 'picky' foods!

We begin to see how other people play a very important part in our lives, and how we are able to unconsciously manipulate getting our own needs met by them. Our size plays a fundamental role in this manipulation: *getting* thin enables us to have all our needs met; *staying* thin does not.

Additionally, as we lose our higher levels of self-worth and self-confidence, prompted by the decreasing attention from others, we create a physical change in ourselves that once again reflects visually what we think of ourselves.

In other words, when we feel 'not so good' about ourselves, we physically bring on an appearance that is not so good: we put weight on. We believe we are not good enough, especially in comparison to other people. We need to be able to 'see' why, and being fat gives us that reason.

There is also a manipulative game we play, putting weight on is really no different than having kept the weight off for some time – no one comments about either. We feel lonely in both situations, and the core belief that we are not being good enough is strengthened.

So we put the weight on so that we can then go through the diet process again and begin to get our needs met with positive attention. (We must note that this is not conscious: we are not aware of doing this. However, as you read this book your awareness will grow, and once again I state that you then will have choice.)

So it is hardly surprising that we do not stay thin, because in the long term, there is not much to be gained, and there is really no fun in it, both from a conscious and an unconscious aspect:

- We think we can only eat like rabbits,

- We have to control ourselves all the time around food,

- We think that we have to always be sensible,

- We get absolutely no attention,

- There is no praise given to us,

- Life is empty because we have no project like a diet to keep us occupied, or pre-occupied.

- We are normal, and who really wants to be that… what ever that is?

In fact, it all seems really quite boring and, yes, lonely.

This is not, however, the end of it. There is another way – as long as we open our minds and our thoughts, and begin to embrace change.

In the next chapter we look at another type of therapy, Cognitive Behavioural Therapy (CBT). The basis of this therapy is that we change our thinking so that our behaviour changes. This is something we have already begun to look at in the part on the workings of the brain, and how our expectations and thoughts create our behaviour.

**"THE EASIEST PERSON
TO FOOL IS
YOURSELF!"**

**"SPEAK FROM THE
HEART:
IT`S RISKY
IT`S UNREHEARSED
IT`S SPONTANEIOUS
BUT IT`S HONEST!"**

Chapter Four

THE PERSONALITY

Now that we are aware of so much more around this issue of weight, and food, and how we eat, we will understand that we need to look further. We need to look deeper into ourselves for those long-lasting answers.

Let us not get put off by this, but see it as a way of empowering ourselves. With greater awareness, we will be more able to make the choices that will truly benefit our lives and therefore release us from this obsession and frustration around our weight.

In the quest to look deeper, we shall now look at a certain type of personality we fall into. However, let it be quite clear that although we fall into this type of personality, we also have our own sense of self, with our individuality influencing how it affects us, it does not mean we are all `clones`. We are quite naturally individuals in our own right, and still have ourselves, our own genes that make us uniquely the Anne, Sam, or Lynn we are.

So although we will identify a type of personality we fall into, we behave according to the influence of our own mannerisms within that type. This will become clearer as we read on.

Personality Typing

So who are we? And what is our belief system, our thinking process, that we see acted out through our relationship with food and weight?

Although we are most definitely our own self, it can be said that our type of personality can fall into a certain category. This category will give us many answers, empower us to understand, as well as give us a structure and clarity to produce change.

So what type of personality are we talking about?

The Borderline Personality

Let us try to keep an open mind with this information. Understandably, there might well be anxieties. Let us not let these emotions overwhelm so that we stop reading the book. Finding out new things can be uncomfortable, and it can also be exciting.

We can refer to a book that stands as a bible to psychologists, psychiatrists, and all those specialists that deal with the mental side of the human being. ('Mental'…. Let us educate ourselves as to the real meaning of 'mental'. It has to do with the mind, or means 'in the mind', and that is all that it means!)

The book is called the DSM, *The Diagnostic and Statistical Manual of Mental Disorders.* In other words, it is a book that examines the different ways of different people, clarifies how people function and then identifies what clinical, social or psychological intervention would be supportive if any at all is required. This could be seen as a very 'heavy' book however in essence it does what we all like things to do, it provides answers. There have been several editions, for as our knowledge of the mind and brain increases, the book has been added to and kept up to date.

All recognised conditions are in this book – from minor depression, eating disorders, and schizophrenia, to Parkinson's disease, sleep disorders, and anxieties.

However, we are only looking at 'borderline personality' and using the 'bible' to do so. What better reference point could we have?

The DSM IV has much to say about everything, it is that sort of book .

Three quotes that stand out for me would be:

'there is instability in personal relationships and self-images as well as a noticeable impulsiveness in behaviour`

'individuals will appear to 'do' anything to avoid real, or imagined, abandonment.`

'may be troubled by chronic feelings of emptiness, are easily bored and therefore constantly seek something to do.`

There is obviously much more than this written about the Borderline Personality, and we could go into it extensively. However, for us to make sense of it in relation to ourselves and our food issues, we need to attend to crucial points so that we can keep focussed on the areas that matter the most and see the resemblance between us and this type. So let us start with how we view ourselves. In other words, who are we, how do we feel, and how do we identify ourselves?

Vulnerable

This is not a word that we accept of ourselves comfortably, and our first reaction to this would be that this is nonsense. However, if we take time to think, we are able to realise that we accept what others say; even if we do not agree, we keep quiet and are found to go along with the crowd, for an easy life.

We do this because we want others to like us. The thought is that if others are happy, then we can be happy because we feel liked by them, and this is important to us. Unfortunately, we believe this depends on us doing a lot for them, so the relationship becomes conditional, and therefore very sensitive and fragile; the burden lies on our ability to please, which puts us in a position of being vulnerable.

Betrayed

We often feel betrayed by other people's responses to what we do, as they often seem unfair. We can so easily end up thinking they do not appreciate what we do – all the effort and hard work we put in` and they barely even notice.

Dominated

Other people's needs seem to play a very large part in our thinking. Not only do we worry about what they are thinking, we often imagine what they might be thinking, and act in a way that corresponds to these imagined thoughts.

What other people want seems to be much more important than what we want, if indeed we even know what we want... outside of wanting people to like us.

It now becomes obvious to us that there is a very strong theme developing .... We appear to be caught up with other people!

Deprived

We constantly deprive ourselves from receiving any emotional support, which is interesting because, we really want emotional support and to feel nurtured. In fact, we experience a sense of emptiness when our expectations are not met on this level.

Clearly there is a conflict here: we want and expect support, but instead deprive ourselves from receiving any.

Why would we do this?

When we relate to our physical side, and the size we are, it becomes obvious how this happens. Being fat is something we feel very uncomfortable with, and it leads us to dislike ourselves. In that self-disliking place, we find it very difficult to accept that other people will like us, or like how we look, let alone want to become intimate with us. So our fat becomes a barrier for us; it keeps us to ourselves, and it keeps people out, which might sound a good trade–off. However, we then become isolated and deprived of emotional sharing.

For ourselves, we find it hard to accept that any emotion other than happiness is allowed. Whenever we feel unhappy, irritated, frustrated, or uncomfortable, we think this is wrong; we think others will not want to know us; and we think we are bad people when we feel and show any of these emotions, so we keep ourselves to ourselves, and in so doing this we feed.

Any emotion felt outside of the degree that feels manageable we feed. We exacerbate those emotions by doing something that we can then feel bad about, we eat inappropriately which adds to feeling bad about the emotions we had to begin with. The only relationship, therefore, that we turn to in difficult times is the one we have with food. And yet food cannot give us what we really need. (This refers back to euphoric recall, where we still think food can give us a metaphorical hug!)

Powerless

As our attention is nearly always focussed on others and what they want, we could say that they pull all the strings, and we would not be far wrong. This does place us in a powerless position, because it is the needs of the others that influence us, that have the power to dictate.

This is extremely noticeable when we look at our relationship with food. Often we think that as long as the food isn't in the house we will be OK. This noticeably gives power to the food and places us in a very weak position in regard to it.

As mentioned before, we see other thin people as 'lucky' and think 'It's not fair – I just have to look at food and I put weight on!'

All of these thoughts illustrate for us beautifully how powerless we are.

Out of Control

Naturally, if others have the power and we are powerless, then we are not in full control of our lives. This is often felt around food. It seems that when others say jump, we merely say 'how high?' rather than wondering if we in fact want to jump at all. The ability to feel in control and have our own choices in life, to fulfil our own needs, feels very limited. To say the word 'no" is just so difficult!

And last, probably the most important view of ourselves is:

Not Feeling Good Enough

Incredibly difficult is it for us to think that we are important, that we are the person that matters.

We visually act this out too, because of the weight we carry.

Who would want to love us and see us as good when we are so 'horrid' to look at?

When we were young we picked up signals, messages that have left us feeling not very good about ourselves, and our relationship with food illustrates this for us quite clearly.

We mentioned earlier of how we eat in a self -harming way. We almost go into self-destruct mode around food and can think, 'Who cares? I'm fat anyway.' Or 'What's the point? I'm useless.'

We eat to the point of shear discomfort sometimes, to the point of bursting. We would not do this if we honoured our bodies, if we looked after ourselves and felt we were worth looking after.

We lack that self-importance and self-value, if you will, that self-esteem and confidence, and whilst that is not present we are left with feelings of uselessness and despair.

In short, we do not feel good enough about ourselves.

So the view of ourselves is not a good one. We could now be feeling even more fed up, for this recognition and awareness of self can be depressing. However, this information is offered to you to give you power, to give you some control, and to give you choice: if we understand more, then we can help ourselves.

We have touched a little on how we see ourselves. Now let us briefly make a similar list for others so that we can make a comparison and give ourselves some structure. So how do we view other people?

Ideal

We tend to put them on a pedestal and think that they always get it right. What they do, and how they do things, is the better way.

They live in the ideal way, the choices they make are the better ones, and they know so much more than us… and so the thoughts go on.

Especially when these other people are thin, we impose all sorts of thoughts on to them: about how lucky they are and how they appear to be 'in control', this being something we admire hugely, especially around food.

We can also see how we feed into this belief. When we socialise with others, we often find ourselves eating similar foods, or asking what they might be choosing to eat – as if what they do is something to follow, the better choice to make!

Powerful

Remember how we let others do what they want and follow their desires? This goes hand in hand with our own sense of powerlessness. We can also place food in the category of 'others', in so far as it has all the power over us… as soon as we see it, we truly believe we must eat it.

'Powerful', 'pedestal' and 'ideal' all have the same connotations for us, and can be placed in the same 'box'.

Devaluing

Ironically, although we give other people all of the afore mentioned traits, we also see them as people who do not give us what we need. The support and the nurturing that we believe in some way we deserve are never given to us, and therefore we can easily see from this aspect that they do not `come up to scratch`.

Consequently we feel let down by them and devalue them because of that experience.

They never seem to notice exactly how much effort we put into pleasing them, and because of this we often feel taken for granted, which in itself is highly devalues them.

Rejecting, Betraying, Controlling, and Abandoning

In the long term, and therefore in the short term, too, we do see others as being hurtful.

By placing them on a pedestal, we give them admiration, and we expect them to respond in a way that shows appreciation and gratitude for all the things we do and how we care for them.

This, however, is merely our own perspective of our relationship, our own beliefs of how the other person needs to betaken care of. This is not verbally communicated to us by them; it is a path we travel silently in the belief that we know what needs to be done, and what other people need.

Our reality is harsh, others do not realise our own viewpoint on life because of our silence, they do not respond, they cannot respond because they have no idea of what is `going on` for us, and so they are seen as rejecting us and our work, and betraying the relationship (which we have imposed on them, with our conditions of 'giving' and 'doing.)

In doing this, we give others the control, and the power, and what becomes most important to us is their acknowledgement of how we care about and work hard for them. Thus that lack of response is interpreted by us as needing to do more or even that what we have done is not good enough. Their lack of response touches on our very sensitive 'spot' of not feeling good enough about ourselves, never getting things quite right, we turn around their lack of response onto ourselves, because that is what we do!

In essence, their lack of acknowledgement of us and our 'doing' is interpreted by us as a form of abandonment.

No wonder we keep hold of our fat that protects us and gives us an excuse for people being like this. It acts as a buffer against a world that appears to over-look us completely.

Further on in this chapter, I will write these points down so that we can see it altogether.

These differing views of ourselves and others result in us having certain beliefs, which we shall proceed to look at:

Cannot Cope with Being on Our Own and with Being Disliked

We want people to like us. More than this, we absolutely need for people to like us. When other people ignore, or overlook us, the affect is devastating. We become overwhelmed by this experience of abandonment and can find ourselves thinking about it for the whole day, often pulling other people into our experience to see what they might say. The affect is huge, and we become very troubled by the situation.

We think we cannot cope on our own!

Let's be careful here that we do not reject this out of hand. Of course, we are able to cope with life – after all we run homes, keep a job down, and go 'out to play'. But we need to look at our emotional self and realise how much we need others to like us.

We need people to be around in that friendly way, for people to think we are good, for us all to get on. The thought of disagreements, arguments, and confrontation scares us skinless. For us to experience 'bad' feelings, or think that others might be experiencing them weighs heavily, and we do not feel we are 'enough' on our own.

We Need Someone to Rely On

What now emerges is some conflict. We need others, want others, and yet when we rely on them we become upset, as they never seem to give us enough, which leaves us feeling hurt.

Yet to say anything of our hurt, to voice our needs, we believe would cause such problems and disharmony. So we struggle on, keeping quiet, and believing that we just need to 'do' one more thing, and then they will notice.

We need that other person to recognise us; we rely on them to give us our 'feel good factor'. We do not feel good enough, so we are unable to give ourselves this message because we do not value ourselves.

We Cannot Bear Unpleasantness

We so want all the time for everyone to be happy, happy, happy. For every one to smile and get along with each other. And we will 'do' anything to try to have that situation.

If We Rely on Someone, We Will Find Ourselves Mistreated, Found Wanting and Abandoned

Those other people just do not get it; they do not give us the nurturing, the notice, the gratitude, nor the appreciation and thanks, so we feel lonely.

The Worst Possible Scenario Would Be to Be Left and Abandoned

The thought of being disliked, ignored and not spoken to is too overwhelming, too catastrophic for us and the feelings of discomfort around this are believed to be far too unmanageable.

We Deserve to Be Punished

When we do not feel good enough, we believe we deserve all manner of bad things.

We can certainly see this thought, this belief, being acted out through the food that we eat. After all, putting weight on is punishing to us.

The way we choose to live creates a struggle for us, this serves to punish us and keep that easy life away from our grasp.

Adding all of these together – our view of ourselves, our view of others, and the beliefs that we have – we will naturally have worked out some strategies for surviving:

Our Strategies for Survival

1. We put our own needs to the back of the queue. In other words, we overlook what we need and concentrate on the needs of others.

It is when we are in the very moment of recognising this that we eat.

2. When we are stressed, we relieve tension through self-mutilation and self-destructive behaviour.

For all the reasons that we have just read about, our lives are stressful. All it takes is one little thing for us to tip over the edge and find ourselves eating our 'picky' foods.

Eating in the way that we do – copious quantities and until we feel sick, bloated, and have to undo our zip – when we are not hungry *is* self-destructive, and it does mutilate, because we gain weight in a way that can almost disfigure us.

We would only be doing this if we felt we were not good enough.

3. We wait until we can no longer tolerate the feelings of being ignored, and then we blow. We become very punitive towards those who have overlooked our hard efforts and become very passionate in our protest, it is at times like these that we realise we are in the kitchen feasting for England because we have been overlooked one too many times and the urge to get back at that other person becomes solely focussed upon the food.

Marsha Lineham, writes of the Borderline Personality,

`We often over-commit to others to maintain approval from them`

`By putting the other person first, more often than not, we as individuals will be negating our own needs,`

`Just as relationships will 'blow up' if unattended, at times an individual will 'blow up' if priorities and demands in life are unattended and not balanced.`

For us, the 'blow up' is usually our time of eating.

So we have a view of self, a view of others, the beliefs these cause us to have, and the strategies that enable us to survive.

If we return to Eric Berne's Transactional Analysis, we will see a lot of our Critical Parent in our view of self and our view of others.

The Critical Parent – with her talk of 'should', 'ought', 'must', 'have to', 'got to', 'be polite', 'keep others happy' – is saying that the needs of everyone else are more important.

The Critical Parent, although an ego state of our own, is also present in others, and comes from external sources, too – even our own mothers. Mothers are probably the most important Critical Parent we have. Other powerful people talk in this way, too, and we listen to them, and allow them to meet their needs first, whilst ours are less important. This would be our Adaptive Child acting out.

Many a time we were told when we were young, 'Be good, and be polite, because then they will like you, and you might get invited back.' Such a loaded comment for us to hear. Were we ever told to enjoy ourselves, have some fun, or even to take care? No, it was always about looking after our host. We would do our best to oblige and show we had been brought up correctly, playing the role of the Adaptive Child.

However, every so often we have the urge to give back to ourselves, and at this point our Rebellious Child 'will out'. This would be Marsha Lineham's 'blow up' moment. Whilst seeing the world as unfair – feeling a victim, and thinking no one cares – we turn to food, or maybe alcohol and in truth 'cut our nose to spite our face', we feed into that strategy of self-destruction and self-mutilation.

All of these reasons and different schools of therapy, however, can easily be seen as the same actions being taken for the same type of reasons. Historically, we now know we use food because it was offered to us as a treat in our childhood, and because we still think it will give us that warm, wonderful, metaphorical hug, and that it will make us feel better, when the reality is that once we've eaten, swallowed the food we always wish we never had.

So let's summarise our Borderline Personality.

Here we are being:

Vulnerable
Betrayed
Dominated
Deprived
Powerless
Out of control
Unable to feel good about ourselves

Other people are:

Idealized
Powerful
Devaluing
Rejecting
Betraying
Controlling
Abandoning
... In other words, hurtful, although they do not mean to be.

It needs to be emphasised that this is not about seeing other people as bad because they have been placed in a superior position.

We must acknowledge that this is what we do ourselves. Without being asked, or told, we place others first, for reasons that are our own.

Our main beliefs are that:

- We cannot cope on our own.

- We need someone to rely on.

- We cannot bear unpleasantness.

- We will find ourselves wanting when we rely on others.

- The worst possible scenario would be to be left and abandoned.

- We deserve to be punished.

… And because of these dynamics, we have three strategies that enable us to manage our lives:

1. Overlook our own needs

2. Have self-destructive and self-mutilating behaviour

3. Be able to be rather punitive to others.

In essence, the world feels a very unkind place, with us struggling in it, and seeing everyone as so much better off than us. In fact, it is because of this view that we can almost see others as the enemy and in that vain we isolate ourselves.

In our isolation we have a lot of internal as well as external battles, which ultimately produce high levels of anxiety and stress. It is as if our lives are built on a foundation of stress, tension and anxiety, so when something extra, or out of our control occurs, we only have a very short fuse left. The unexpected happens, and our fuse sparks off. We are so near the end that we have nothing else to give except the 'ignition', the 'blow up'.

Chaos, so we believe, is so close. We feel eternally on the edge of it, and we push ourselves into attempting to manage more… and more… and yet more. The levels of stress obviously increase, becoming quite extreme, and the only way we believe we can cope is to turn to food.

Once again, in that moment of deep disbelief that we can manage, we eat the foodstuffs that we believe will bring back the will to live, or will hug us metaphorically.

Let's face it: although short lived, we do experience that moment fully and intensely, and the food does provide relief from the stress and strain of this difficult and very full life. However, what we are really doing is fulfilling a strategy, a survival mechanism, **and** relieving tension through self-mutilation and self-destructive behaviour.

Once again: food enables behaviour!

What type of behaviour? Food is used

- To treat

- To relieve tension

- To be self-destructive

- To self-mutilate

- To metaphorically hug

- To rebel

- To be 'out of it'… which could be seen as relief, too.

None of these reasons are for hunger. This reason is nowhere to be found. What are we able to conclude from this? Our psychology is absolutely in the way of us allowing food to be just food.

To help us fully understand and experience this new-found knowledge, let us complete the following exercise:

Think of a problematic situation involving yourself and another, and write it down. This could be an isolated incident or an on going situation.

1. Look at the list of how we view ourselves. How do you see yourself in this situation? Powerless? Deprived? Out of control? What are you doing or not doing, and what does this tell you about yourself?

2. How do you see that other person? Powerful? Wonderful? Controlling? I wonder what they are doing in this situation and what you are letting them do?

3. With these inequalities in place, how do you now view the world? For example, unfair, lonely, scary, a struggle...?

Writing this down makes it more real for us. We can 'live' the situation, look at it with an analytical mind, and therefore be more aware, more objective, about it.

Do we see how much of a 'victim' we are to life and life's circumstances?

Let us now look at what we do and why! It is often the case that we have many, many thoughts inside our heads. The thoughts often involve what I call a 'Jackanory' Theme. What do I mean by this? Well, we will impose things on to other people, but they themselves do not have any understanding or awareness of this. For example, 'If I say that, then they will think I mean this, which in turn will cause them to react in that way'.... And so it goes on.

Another example of this would be: 'When I saw Sue today she didn't look very happy. I don't think she liked what I said yesterday, and I think she was upset by what Judy said.'

In each of these examples there is mere supposition being used to attempt to understand something that in reality we know nothing about. What we do whilst using the 'Jackanory' Theme is impose on others our own belief system, our own way of doing things, our own yardstick. At no point have we clarified how Sue feels and why. Instead, we have ourselves being alone with a whole imagined scenario. This does not allow others their way of doing things!

Let us continue by looking into the underlying beliefs – this would be the Jackanory Theme, the beliefs we have that underpin our actions.

4. So in the situation that you have chosen, what do you do? For example, do you keep quiet and then go to another person, friend, and moan about the situation to them. Do you overlook what you would really like to say to the other person within this particular scenario, and just do what the other person wants?

5. In doing this, what do you think, or hope, will happen? What have you thought, all on your own, without checking it out with the other person? For example, do you think that the other person will really appreciate you more, will like you more, will notice you having done whatever it is that you have done, and/or that life will continue to be peaceful?

And then we need to look at what does happen. What is the end result of what you choose to do? For example, no real thanks, still not noticed much, life really isn't easy and quiet, still feeling unloved by that person or disliked.

Now… let's wildly imagine that we do it all differently!

6. What if the alternative were to happen, and you were not so silent, and you put yourself to the front of the queue? For example, you told the other person in this situation how you really did feel. Write down what you would say to them.

7. What do you think would happen? For example, the other

person would hate you, possibly abandon you, think you were a horrible person, or there would be confrontation, shouting, etc.… Or even that you would get ignored.

So now let's summarise, just go through that again, and get it into a format that we can be clear about.

1. What is the situation?

2. How do you feel? And it must be emphasised at this point that we need to recognise exactly how we feel! For example, sad, lonely, angry…

3. How do we see ourselves? Powerless, out of control, vulnerable…

4. How do we see others? Powerful, betraying, controlling rejecting…

5. How does life seem to us, how does the world seem, in this scenario? (I guess the world is seen as being unfriendly, unfair…)

6. So you …. What do you do? Keep quiet and say nothing.)

7. Then this will happen… (The other person will eventually give me praise and realise how hard I have worked.

8. Now then, is this right? Do you really receive this recognition and praise?

9. Do you get what you really want? Do you get acknowledgement, praise, or a thank you?

10. Do you really want to carry on with the way you manage and experience this type of situation?

If we have really searched hard for the answers to these questions, if we understand what they are asking for, we will see that they highlight the fact that we do not get what we want at all!

The strategy of putting our own needs to the back of the queue, of keeping quiet, of leaving everything to telepathy and hope, does not give us what we want or deserve.

We could do what we do well: judge ourselves harshly for doing this. This would be the Critical Parent. It would be kinder to turn to the Nurturing Parent and allow ourselves the thought that we do what we do for good reason.

So we do have that Jackanory Theme, we have always had it, and when we were younger, it probably kept us safe in many ways. It meant that we could live with a greater sense of comfort in our lives because we could think that:

- We were liked

- We were well thought of

- We understood the situation

- We felt in control

What stands out in the answers is that we remain in a world heavily populated by ourselves, and only ourselves. This is because we are afraid of what others might do. Put this into context and we remember that we believe we are not good enough when it comes to others.

The confusion we have is that we do not get the outcome that we hope for and fantasize about.

We do loads to help others, but we do not get recognised for it. We experience all sorts of emotions but keep quiet about them, for fear of confrontation.

Always in the hope that one day, there will be a meeting of the different ways... But it never happens.

The missing piece in all of this is that even if others did give us praise and thank us, we would find it incredibly difficult to accept, and our immediate response would be to throw it back in their faces.

How many times has someone said to us 'I like your shirt', only for us to reply 'What, this old thing?' Or 'It only cost a fiver at the market.' We do find it incredibly difficult to accept nice things being said to us, or being done for us... we almost squirm!

Through the exercise we have just done, we realise this way of doing things does not work for us at all; in fact, it harms us rather than benefits us, but that's OK to make this realisation because now we know this we can change things.

Are we able to make the connection between this way of being and how we behave with food?

We are very isolated people and because our level of communication around the more appropriate subject of ourselves and how we feel, what we are thinking, is at a minimum, we have a raised and dysfunctional relationship with food.........because it has become a friend to us in this isolation.

It has become our Metaphorical Hug.

Another factor that plays into this personality type would be extreme thinking.

Extreme Thinking

We tend to see everything in life and everyone in life in one category or another, and to prove this to ourselves we can make two lists, one with the heading of 'Good' and the other with 'Bad'. Underneath each heading write words that tally with those categories:

Good

Thin
Relaxed
Tall
Busy
Unselfish
Kind
Caring
Happy

... The list continues.

Bad

Fat
Stressed
Short
Lazy
Selfish
Unkind
Uncaring
Depressed

... Once we start we can go on forever, because there is always a word that fits the judgement of good or bad.

We can clearly see this within our life of dieting, too.

We have constantly been bombarded with very strong views of what foods are good and bad. There are even words such as 'sin' branded to certain foods. 'Free' is another word used.

We wake in the morning and tell ourselves we are 'going to be good'. Unfortunately, as we say this to ourselves we are giving ourselves permission to be bad. This is because when one extreme is put in place, the only other direction we can go in is the other extreme.

The tension we impose on ourselves with this thought is huge. The Adaptive Child endeavours rigorously to apply, to adapt, and to conform, and yet understandably on many an occasion we become too stressed with these absolutes. Hanging in the wings is the rebel in us that wants to let go of the whole thing and relax, but when extremes are all that we have, there is an inability to just relax – we swing into letting go in a big way and therefore become 'bad'!

The answer to this, of course, is to live in the middle ground, which is not so easy to define, and for many of us it appears too wishy-washy to even begin to believe that this is a good place to take up. After all, there is no great achievement in noticing that the middle appears to have no direction, and it might even be quite boring.

What sort of words could we apply to the middle ground in the case of food? For instance,

- 'Food is just food.'

- 'I shall not have a good day or a bad day. The day will be what it needs to be, and I shall eat what I choose to eat.'

This feels very different for us. Hopefully, we will be insightful enough to realise that these types of thoughts and statements produce a freer attitude – we can be neither good nor bad because we have allowed ourselves to let go of the judgements. We thus give ourselves permission to just be who we are.

We cannot be bad people because we are not really being good people, after all who is who to make the absolute statement of 'you are a good person!' Across the whole personality structure it would be almost impossible to make a conclusive statement of 'you are a bad person' this is an extreme statement and therefore is not an honest comment.

Once we get in touch with this 'middle' place, we are able to feel very liberated – the lessened judgement is so up-lifting.

Part of the Borderline Personality is that we find it difficult to change. We are very stuck in our ways and have a huge disbelief that we are able to do anything and do any `changing`.

So let us endeavour to be kind to ourselves and allow all of this new understanding to ruminate within for a time before we begin to think that we can just up sticks and change.

"WHEN WE TRY TO
POSESS
SOMEONE ELSE WE END
UP GRASPING EMPTINESS"

"A MUTUAL EXCHANGE
AND SHARING
OF IDEAS, THOUGHTS
AND FEELINGS
IS THE BEST WAY TO
BUILD A
RELATIONSHIP"

Chapter Five

THE THOUGHTS OF A VICTIM

It's quite a revelation for us to read that we are a particular personality type. This can be uncomfortable for us to learn, but it can be liberating for us to know at last that there is hope, because there are answers, albeit not the type of answers we have been looking for.

After the last chapter, let us be clear about the differences between us and others: crudely stated we are 'unimportant and alone, powerless and not good enough', whilst others are 'big, important, powerful, and people who get things – and life – right"

If we turn our attention to the theory of the Drama Triangle, we will have another piece of theory that can reinforce our learning so far, and for those of us that are possibly confused this might bring some clarity.

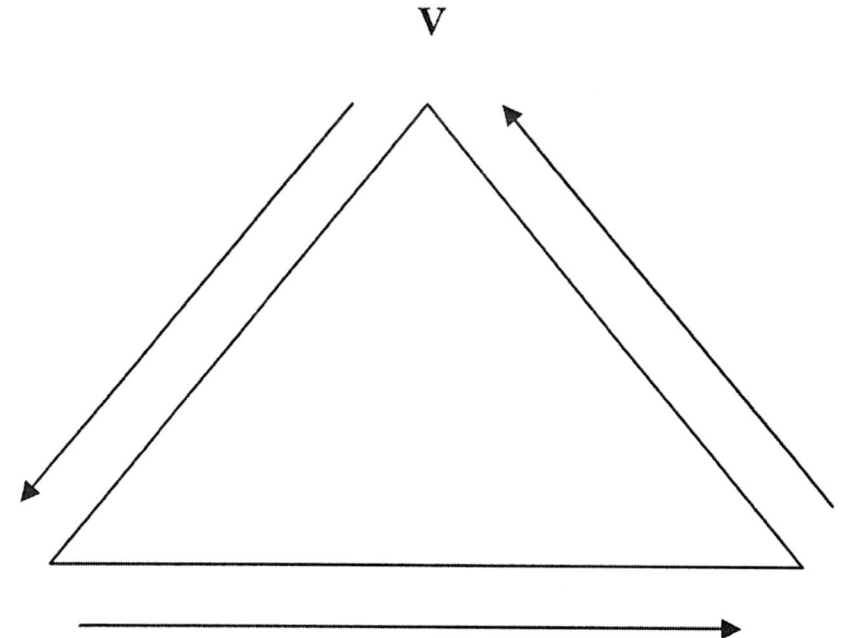

The 'V' stands for Victim.

The 'R' stands for Rescuer.

The 'P' stands for Persecutor.

As Borderline Personalities, our view of ourselves most definitely fits into the Victim position. In the same way as Eric Bernes Transactional analysis has the Critical Parent in both ourselves and others so we can also hold the Rescuer Position as well as the Victim, however the other positions are very transitory whilst the ever pervading sense of being a victim is far more pronounced to us.

We view others as `being right` we position them in the powerful place of a Rescuer, because we look up to them. We see them as having all the answers and therefore the ability to help us.

Let us put this theory into context and apply it to the subject of our fat, or weight, and/or dieting.

We feel that we are a Victim of our fat, and often find ourselves thinking: 'It's not fair. I can't help this size. It doesn't matter what I eat – I am born to be big, all I have to do is look at food and I gain weight…'

In essence, we can clearly see that we feel sorry for ourselves, so we are in that 'poor me' position, the Victim position.

So we go along to some 'Diet Club', with the viewpoint, or expectation, or the hope, that they, the people running it, will rescue us, that they will free us from this Victim place and make us thin and happy once again!

We obviously take our Borderline Personality to the Diet Club, too, which supports the Critical Parent, Adaptive Child dynamic (going along with that being 'powerless, out of control and feeling not good enough' stuff) and wait to be told what to do by the Critical Parent, or otherwise by people that are 'powerful', 'in control', and who know best, in this instance by the Rescuers.

The people running the diet regime, for reasons we do not need to go into, collude with this and communicate to us from a Critical Parent position, a position of authority and rescuing, and tell us what we 'should' do and eat, how many points to consume in a day, or how to separate foods by colours, and what ever else there is out there.

We give the 'diet people' all this power. We look up to them and believe that they are in some perfect position and have no issue with food. So we follow what they say, not really thinking for ourselves, because to think for ourselves would interfere with the path of success. They become our Rescuers, to our Victim place and we act as the Adaptive Child and follow the dot of the 'I' and the cross of the 'T', reflecting our sense of powerlessness, feeling out of control, and thinking that we are not good enough.

Inadvertently, what begins to happen is that the Adaptive Child part of us eventually participates in the diet, to 'please' the Critical Parent, in the hope that we shall receive some type of praise. The relationship becomes distorted, and the person running the diet regime becomes a person to be accountable to and to please. And that becomes the issue, rather than losing weight for ourselves.

Possibly more apparent to us are the memories of how we would go to 'the meeting', lose one lb. or so, and then sneakily treat ourselves to fish and chips or a kebab on the way home, with the thought that we have the whole week to lose the weight we think this 'cheating' meal has put on us. This would be the Rebellious Child reacting to the type of relationship we have with the diet people.

In the case of the 'Drama Triangle' we whizz round the triangle as if there is no tomorrow, acting the Victim we attend the weekly diet class, hoping for the Rescue, doing as we are told, almost, we follow the rules of the rescuer, however the time comes when we reject their advice and start to persecute them for the fact that we do not want to carry on listening to them, this is when we go to the 'chippie' and have that disallowed meal.

Respectfully said, if we stayed in a more adult state, we would realise that the cheating is non-beneficial for us. We are the ones that lose out, because our weight is our weight, and if we want to lose it, then the cheating is not helping us.

As we know, the 'treat' comes from our euphoric recall, which tricks us into thinking that we love the food. The reality of the behaviour is that we will eat too much of whatever we choose, which transfers the occasion into a punishment.

Going back to the Drama Triangle, we resume our position of Victim, seeking help from the Rescuer. However, when the desired result does not come to fruition, which in this case is weight loss, we then start to blame the diet club for being useless. We have thoughts such as 'Their system is awful. What is the point of going when we only lose half a pound or a pound? It's too slow; we can't possibly live like this.'

The people who run the club continue to talk to us with the Critical Parent vocabulary. In other words, they constantly give us advice: 'You should do this. Try this. You need to do that, Just keep on doing that...'

Our culture is very bound up in offering advice to people – in the hope that we can help others. However, as with all advice, it eventually begins to produce feelings of anxiety and pressure for the one being given it. And it defines who is in the better place in life: those that give advice are people who feel better than those they offer advice to.

The true outcome of advice is that it serves to exacerbate the feelings we have anyway of not being good enough because we find it too difficult to follow another persons view. Logically this makes sense. The advisors are not us, and their experience is not the same as ours, so it is not natural for us to take on another person's view of life.

This is why some schools of therapy absolutely will not advise, as they believe it is misplaced in its helpfulness!

However, returning to our scenario, eventually this advice takes its toll and we move from Victim to Persecutor because we are now angry, and begin to think: 'The diet people don't seem to understand us; they won't go along with who we are; they don't even know who we are, and their silly diet can go get lost.' We use the strategy of wanting to punish those that show signs of not having what we want (Borderline Personality characteristic).

As a reaction to this, the diet people are moved to the position of Victim. We move them to this position because we experience a momentary belief that we are better than the diet club people. Our thoughts are that they are wrong and we have done our best.

However, in a relatively short period of time, we begin to feel guilty for our behaviour and thoughts because Adaptive Children do not think like this. So we move into the Rescuer position and start to do a lot for them, become subservient to the cause of the diet, and generally struggle on with it all.

Our change in position causes us to make another change for the diet people: we give them importance, and some admiration; we put them back on the pedestal, and make them a Rescuer. We view them as the 'in charge people', and start to see them as being more critical, and let them resume their position of offering advice once again.'

So we go round and round and round on this merry-go–round, moving from Victim to Rescuer to Persecutor, battling and struggling with all the different felt senses.

The fundamental point to this theory of the Drama Triangle is that there are no boundaries; we will always think that we can rescue others by giving advice, and we know subconsciously that being a Victim is a good idea because people will help us. The Persecutor position is the by-product of this type of relationship.

The Drama Triangle, also known as the Persecution Triangle is based on us having a sense of responsibility for how other people feel!

We find it incredibly difficult to allow another person their down times. If we felt comfortable with sadness, confusion, irritation, and all of those so-called negative emotions, we would not hastily go in for the advice giving. We certainly do not do this when people are happy!

People with boundaries allow space between them and others; they are more at ease with those down times, and therefore allow others to go through them. Who are we to infer or judge that they are in the 'wrong' frame of mind? And yet this is what advice does when we are focussed on the emotional level of a person: it directs people to take a different direction, to change what and who they are. We give advice only if a judgement call has been made and the judgement comes up with a negative result.

If we thought that we did not need to rescue others, then others would not go into Victim mode. There would be no point as there would not be an outcome to it. We all know, I'm sure, someone who acts the martyr. Think of how we are around them, always feeling as though we need to tread on egg shells We change how we are to accommodate this somewhat 'helpless' behaviour; we treat them with kid gloves… so the martyrdom works, and these people get their own way, which is the reaction they think they want.

Alternatively, we can overlook this behaviour and carry on in the manner that suits us, which appears to be less attentive to the martyr and on some level might appear to be ignoring such behaviour. Eventually, the martyrdom will out; there is no point to it, nothing special happens. In fact, it sets them apart from us, and this they do not like.

When we are away from the carousal of the Drama Triangle the type of relationship is a lot healthier. Otherwise we go round and round in this triangle, never getting off and always working from either the Victim, Rescuer or Persecutor position.

As we can see, the Borderline Personality supports the Drama Triangle. We naturally give other people that power. The people that run the diet club have a lot of power and appear to be in control. They have all the answers because they run the group sessions all trim and slim, so we put them on a pedestal.

We idealize them!

In comparison, we feel vulnerable – especially around this weight issue – and hope that the diet people will give us all the answers/ Powerless and out of control, we avidly follow the diet without questioning it.

We might even engage in a lot of talking with the diet people, hoping to strike up a special relationship that will give us the titbit of information that will save us.

As time marches on, however, we realise we are not being treated any differently, don't feel special, and the results are not what we want them to be. So we experience a rejection: all those chats have amounted to nothing; we do not receive the special attention that we think we deserve; and the sense of abandonment is painful to us.

Eventually, we act out the strategy we have as Borderline people and use the food to punish those we think have abandoned us.

Returning to the boundary issue, this is a very odd subject for us to think about as it defies all thoughts and beliefs that we have lived with for most of our lives. It contradicts the messages we were given when we were little about being polite and nice so that others will like us and invite us around again. This inadvertently tells us that we can manipulate others and we are responsible for their thoughts.

Because of this, we are now individuals who think we can make others feel happy. We think we can do things to influence other's state of being, which is ironic, considering the fact that we feel so powerless.

However, with this thinking we become enmeshed with others and do not allow them to have their own identity. Remember the Jackanory

Theme: we impose on others what can only be our own way of looking at things. This is constantly being driven by the thought 'I'm only OK, if you're OK'. Conversely, if others are not OK, then we are not OK! So the importance of this is huge.

For us to stand apart from this Drama Triangle and find greater peace and contentment within ourselves is to find our boundaries and consequently allow others theirs. When there is space between us, even those that we love, we will be able to find that sense of self-empowerment, self-worth, and self-value that has evaded us so far.

So the Drama Triangle is where it is.

Not only do we have the Borderline Personality (this is from Cognitive Behavioural Therapy), but we have also the Critical Parent and Drama Triangle (this is from Transactional Analysis). They all amount to the same belief system, which is: 'I'm OK, you're OK', a book in its own right written by Thomas A. Harris. This talks of how we can only feel OK if others feel Ok, reflecting in the fact that we are so caught up with other people rather than having our own identity and our own sense of self regardless of others.

As Cognitive Behavioural Therapy works on the belief that our behaviour (what we do) is a direct result of what we think, we really must look closely at what goes on inside our thinking. We have already touched on this with the Drama Triangle and the Borderline Personality.

We have learnt about our euphoric recall and how we are 'hell bent' on keeping hold of the belief that food is a treat. However, for us to change our behaviour we must change this and other belief systems. The previous chapters have hopefully begun to dislodge our much assumed and projected thinking patterns, because we now know that:

Our behaviour does not get us what we want.

If we return to the exercise we last completed, we can see how we often keep quiet because we believe that others will shout at us and reject us.

Whilst we use this reasoning – and if I may be so bold this excuse – we are not able to be equally present in relationships. This is not helpful for us because by sitting on our reactions, by over looking how we feel about things, we wait for the blow up to happen.

When we believe we have no choice in, and control over, our emotions we instinctively 'let rip', and when we do it will be over the washing up or something trivial. And yet it will not really be about such things.

So how do we think?

Well, our view of ourselves is really quite harmful. We see ourselves as vulnerable, emotionally isolated, out of control, powerless and ultimately not good enough.

In the meantime, we see others as powerful, perfect, having it all, and yet rather controlling, rejecting, abandoning, and betraying. All this makes our world unfair, lonely, and sometimes scary.

As we think in this way, view the world and people as we do, our behaviour will be that of the Victim, and this is wonderfully illustrated by the Drama Triangle.

We can also see this reflected clearly in our weight, our relationship with food, and how we conduct our lives. We think:

- Life is difficult,

- We are never able to have the weight that we want,

- We need to struggle with our weight and with food,

- Whether people are a burden and are the cause for us being stressed so much that we eat,

- We can do, must do, more than others, which is stressful.

- We do not have human limitations and should go on for ever…

The list is endless.

Turning for a minute to the subject of food specifically, let us see how our thoughts affect us. In accordance with Cognitive Behavioural Therapy, there are specific categories in which we place our thoughts. There are:

1. Excuses – we use everything else as the reason to eat.

2. Self-beating – seeing ourselves as hopeless.

3. Demands – this is where the 'should' comes in, and we think it is only polite to eat for others.

So how does this all work?

Let us look at all the situations in which we have a tendency to overeat and see how we think to ourselves in these situations.

1. **Getting home from work,** we walk into the kitchen and without too much thought start opening the fridge, the cupboards, and maybe the wine. We think to ourselves: 'We've had a long day, it's been hard and we deserve something nice.' (Excuse.)

2. **Waking up in the morning, we look at the long day ahead,** and in addition to that long day, everyone in the world tells us we 'should' eat in the morning to start up our metabolism. We think: 'Fuel on the fire, build up our strength for the hours ahead, and besides everyone tells us it is a good time to eat.'(Excuse.)

3. **Everything is done, the end of the day has been reached,** and we sit down, put the TV on, and start to

think about food: We think: 'A little something would be nice now, a little treat whilst I watch either this good movie or this boring program.' (Excuse.)

4. **Driving home from work,** or even as part of our work, the journey is long and the roads full, as usual. We think: 'This is so boring; let's relieve the boredom and eat something interesting like this sweet, to keep our concentration up, keep the sugar levels up and make sure we don't fall asleep. (Excuse.)

5. **We are in a restaurant** and others are choosing three courses. They are also having the gooiest dessert on the menu. We think: 'It's not fair if we don't have one; they are having it, so we'll have the same to join in.' (Excuse.)

We could go on with these types of thoughts; we could find plenty more.

If we classify all of these examples we are able to see how they are all excuses.

These excuses convince us whole-heartedly that we are doing the right thing at the right time and grant us that instant gratification we crave.

So the behaviour continues and we eat with the 'normal' outcome of wishing we never had. Which brings in the self-beating type of thinking:

1. **Having just finished the plate of food in front of us,** because we believe we have to finish everything that is on our plate, even though the portion size was far too big, we think: 'We were only going to eat half of that – we are so useless.' (Self-beating).

2. **We have gone all day with very little food,** because we

think that as long as we keep away from food we are safe. However, at some point in the day we must eat, and when this happens we start off with the 'good foods'' and then progress to the biscuits and the chocolate, if not crisps. This reflects the all-or-nothing behaviour, the extremes. We eventually progress to the 'wrong'' foods in large quantities. We think: 'What is wrong with us? We keep ruining our days. We were going to be so good today, and now I've eaten all of that lot.' (Self-beating.)

3. **We weigh ourselves in the morning;** the scales show weight gain. We think: 'We have no will power. We can't do this anymore, and we feel so fat.' (Self–beating.)

We use our relationship with food to beat ourselves up, to emphasise our belief of being out of control, of being powerless, and of not being good enough.

So food really does become a useful tool for us, and our relationship with it reinforces our thoughts about ourselves.

If we look at our lives outside of the food arena, we will also see that our thinking process is exactly the same. For instance, when we have worked really hard at something **we wait** for some acknowledgement from another person, which will validate our arduous work and confirm that the completion of it is 'right' and 'good'. It seems only polite that we receive this commendation; we would certainly give it to another. In fact, we would offer overwhelming gratitude if anyone helped us or even just worked hard.

As we have now found, this does not really happen very often if at all. So what do we do instead of communicating this? We keep quiet and treat ourselves with food!

Amidst this, we find it incredibly hard to find for ourselves the approval we search for from others, and the conclusion we always arrive at is that what we have done is not good enough, and we beat ourselves up for not doing a good enough job, because the absence of notice from others leaves us with nothing else to think.

The last category, demands, is an interesting one and reflects the Critical Parent type of communication.

We live our lives believing that others think the right way and the better thoughts.

We do what others say it is the better thing to do.

So we 'must' eat our breakfast because others say so, regardless of the fact that when we begin eating we cannot stop, so when we eat as early as the morning, the whole day can be a day-long binge!

As long as we 'do' something, we shall be OK, and we will not be deemed 'lazy'. Sitting down and relaxing is something other people are allowed to do, but not us. So when it comes to sitting down in front of the TV we find it incredibly difficult. It is in that 'doing nothing' category, and we have a hard time doing that.

So when we sit down, we think about the 101 things still to do and are irritated with ourselves for not doing them. But now is the time to sit down because we **need** to, we **should** do it to be with the family.

The resistance to relaxing is overwhelming, so the way we manage it is to eat.

Being bored is irritating to us, frustrating, and emotionally rather scary, so in these uncomfortable moments, there is a huge draw, a **need**, to do something to distract us.

So we eat in the car, especially when it stands still in a traffic jam! That is an example of how desperate we can become with this 'not doing' thing.

We like doing what others suggest. Whatever they want to do is the thing to agree with. We eliminate our ideas by so following another's; hence when it comes to going out, we join in with what others eat –their experience of the night out will be the best, and to have the same result we **need** to eat the same.

We could almost label these demands as Associative Eating. When we are in the car, we eat wine gums; when we watch the TV we eat biscuits; when we come home from work we eat cheese. And so it continues. The association is extremely demanding: we find it incredibly difficult to do one thing without the other, and that in itself becomes a huge drive and a huge demand on us.

If we are able to examine the type of foods that we eat we will find that there are certain foods eaten at certain times and in association with specific things in the environment, as mentioned before, sweets only in the car, biscuits are eaten in the evening in front of the TV where as cheese is the food consumed when returning home from a days work.

After all for some of us chocolate cannot be eaten in the morning, where as biscuits before dinner is almost revolting so we find there is a certain etiquette around food.

The most recognisable train of thought that we have around our eating is in the excuse category: we find many an excuse in order that we can act and behave in life in the way that we do and the behaviour of eating is caught up in this.

Let us see how our thinking affects our behaviour with food:

1. When we do things in our life we start them with the belief that there is no other option but to then finish them. We are so adamant about this that we often do not even attempt things because we are fearful that we might not be able to finish them. The start to finish belief is strong.

So we start to eat the plate full of food and we finish the whole plate of food!

2. We have extreme thoughts, it is all or nothing` for us. When we change something it is a radical alteration. When we look at life every thing in it is either good or bad, right or wrong, there is no middle ground.

Even when the days weather has had some sun, but rains for the most, we then 'club' it all together and label the day as 'bad'.

So we tend to see the days consumption of food in extremes, we eat no food or lots of food and the lots of food is viewed as the 'bad' food, to boot.

Even when there has been some of the 'good' food eaten and there have been times amongst the lots of food when food was not eaten, we still tend to generalise and generalise negatively.

3. Giving all the power to other people, seeing them as the perfect measure to go with reinforces this I'm OK, you're OK dynamic.

The scales dominate our lives; we allow these metal objects to give us our 'feel good factor', if they give us a reading we want then we are OK and if they give a reading we do not like we are irritated, the scales have the 'power' to give us a 'good' day!

Something outside of ourselves is seen as having the power to dominate us.

As we have mooted previously, we cannot separate our thinking around food from how we think elsewhere in life. This is absolutely crucial to the message of this book: diets have not really worked because they focus on us changing our thinking around food. This is not going to work for us because we are asking ourselves to be two different people with two different ways of thinking, and that just doesn't happen.

We think about food as we do because we think about life in this way! Our food issues merely highlight our whole thinking process.

It is just so easy to see our behaviour around food and gain the clarification about it.

So we have to alter the thinking *per se* for our food behaviours to change.

One other thought that is not useful for us, in some ways, is what I call 'pink and fluffy' thinking.

'Have she gone mad?' we now ask ourselves. However, read on before making that judgement and extreme thinking comes to fruition.

Because we have the Child in us (Eric Berne's Transactional Analysis), we will have thoughts that correspond to childhood experiences. We often read of fairy tales, of princes on white horses coming to save us and make us into a princess, of how life always – and it was always – ended ``happily ever after'.

We have this expectation still: we always hope that life will work out for us in that way, that happily ever after way, and yet to date we can see that life in the real world is not about princes and princess, or with knights in shining armour: it is what it is – what we make it to be.

Whilst we are unable to relegate this 'pink and fluffy' in our childhood days and relish the innocence and the freedom of them, we are dominated by it more than we recognise and more than is helpful.

Our thoughts are driven by the expectations we have stored in our Filing System. The euphoric recall we have with food is indicative of the euphoric recall of life: it is the 'pink and fluffy' we held as a child.

Do we, I wonder, do things in life for the pink and fluffy outcome? Apart from wedding days, maybe not – or at least apparently not – because we are able to be more adult in our reasoning.

In the case of food, we stay in that child-like place and hold a very believable expectation (euphoric recall) that food will give us something above and beyond what it is able to give us. We become emotionally involved with the expectation which leads us to 'do'' the eating.

When we are able to be more adult with food, we will link the reality of food to the outcome; we will be more accountable with it. In essence, we shall be able to see that four bars of chocolate will give us feelings of being sick, as well as make us gain weight.

When we let go of the `pink and fluffy` which does rather reinforce the helpless place and the Victim position, we realise that we can be equal to others, and know that our way of living is the best way for us, we have boundaries and our own accountability.

Our euphoric recall has food in a pink and fluffy place, our filing system continues to provide memories that reinforce its apparent magical qualities of being able to provide that `happy ending`.

Once we let go of the fairy tale around food and realise the true outcome of over eating we shall empower ourselves to have a far more beneficial relationship with food resulting in an outcome we truly want.

We shall be able to be strong for ourselves and give ourselves what we need, thus letting go of the importance of food and of others. As far as people are concerned they do not have a clue as to where we are coming from, because we do not communicate effectively with them. (This is something we look into towards the end of the book.)

So Let's Now Put It All Together!

Let us collect some of these strands together and see where we can go with it.

The Rebellious Child, in her 'tantrum state, will 'cut off her nose to spite her face' – no real accountability, no good reasoning. She wants to punish everyone for herself having been the otherwise Adaptive Child for too long. Keeping quiet has served no purpose but to cause frustration.

The Rebellious Child fights back at the Critical Parent, with everything she has, and when it comes to food it will be the extreme thinking of lots of bad food.

Obviously, in more lucid moments we will be aware of giving ourselves lots of excuses as to why we can eat what we do eat.

What are excuses? They are reasons based on distorted beliefs that are being manipulated to serve the individual, enabling them to have their own way.

We so want to hit back and eating food lets us do just that.

We have been 'good' for so long, eaten 'healthily', and controlled our urges – doing what our Critical Parent has told us to do, being the virtuous Adaptive Child for so long. This has no other outcome but to introduce the Rebellious Child in a larger–than–life type of way, because there comes this point where we have had enough.

Marsha Lineham calls this the 'blow up'' moment, where life and people all become too much. We feel a great need to let go of being the 'proper' type of person – and this is not only around food but elsewhere also in life – and want to be radical in every which way.

The view of self – of how we feel powerless and out of control – is part of the Child ego. And our view of others – having them on a pedestal, idealizing them as someone perfect – is us looking up to them as a Child would look up to an Adult. This makes the world unfair.

So we let go around our eating. We are adults and we have done our stint with the childhood days, the days of having to do as been told to do and yet still the 'pink and fluffy' doesn't seem to have happened. How annoying is that! So let's eat and be damned to this world!
We have this crooked thinking around food because we have it in life, and once again, the relationship we have with food is merely reflective of that.

There are many levels of our thinking, so this might all be a little confusing. At the same time, hopefully there will be a much greater awareness for us as to how and why we have the relationship with food that we have.

What Are the Levels and How Can We Be Clear?

We have deep-rooted thoughts that stem from our Borderline Personality, that are truly fundamental to our sense of being. They are thoughts about ourselves and how life works – or doesn't – work for us, the emotionally binding relationship we have with others, the world, and food.

We isolate ourselves with our fat because we believe that we are safe in that isolation. Remembering how we are apparently unequal to others, keeping away from them leaves us more peaceful… but alone!

We rarely feel OK about going out to meet with others because we feel the discomfort of our size, and therefore want to hibernate, never really wanting to go out. As we have discovered, we always keep quiet because our belief is that we will cause a confrontation if we voice ourselves.

So in our silence we think and we think too much.

We make up lots of things in our heads, thoughts that we project onto others, feelings that we also project onto others. (This is what I call the Jackanory Theme.) These beliefs become overwhelming, and we become completely convinced that our Jackanory thoughts and perceptions are totally true and absolute fact.

Yet we never really check them out, or clarify their accurateness, which leaves us in this unfair world. For instance, remember that time when someone walked passed us and didn't say hello? Remember how we thought up so many reasons as to why she ignored us:

'We didn't say we liked what she was wearing.'

'We didn't help her the other day when we saw her struggling with her shopping.'

'It's because we're fat and she doesn't want to be seen with us.'

'The way we are is embarrassing for her.'

.... The thoughts go on and on and on. We never really ever think that she just...didn't... see... us. And that is it.

The way we think is so involved; it is intricate, manipulative, distorted, and all–consuming, and always leaves us in a place of feeling down on ourselves, regardless of whether it is around food or people. There are thoughts that originate from our 'filing system' about ourselves and, more recognisably, about food. These come to us from our main carers, the generation before us. We have not only heard the messages but lived through them, too.

Then there are the excuses:

'I'll eat now and make up for it later.'

'This little bit won't hurt.'

'No one will notice if I eat this.'

We come home, or come in from being out somewhere, and we eat and drink because it is a learned behaviour pattern. And that is the excuse: because it is a learned behaviour pattern.

.

Conclusion

There are so, so many involved thoughts, some coming from the core of our very souls and others being superficial, but as with all our thoughts, they produce a behaviour: every behaviour has a thought behind it, and if our behaviour is not biding us well, our thinking needs to be addressed.

Food enables those behaviours.

Our core thoughts have us acting out the strategies of our Borderline Personality. Those core thoughts give us extremely unhelpful behaviours –self-mutilation, self-destruction, and self-silencing, and none of them are good for us.

What we are very aware of is that food is the most useful and accessible tool to use to act these behaviours out.

Strategy – We Subjugate Our Own Needs

We always do so much for other people. We are people-pleasers because we have been brought up to believe that others will like us if we help them. We see others as powerful, more important, and up there on a pedestal, so we will naturally want to follow anyone that we put in that place.

Unfortunately, the way we do this is to the detriment of ourselves. When we become closer to the 'blow up' place, the stress is overwhelming, and so we feed, and often claim an identity around this by saying to others that we eat when we are stressed.

Strategy – Relieve Tension Through Self-Mutilation and Self-Destructive Behaviour

The act of overlooking our own needs and wants creates stress, tension, and impatience at levels that are very high.

It feels as though we live on the edge most of the time anyway, so all it takes is just one extra thing, and we see it as the 'straw that broke the camels back'. For example, someone not saying hello when we thought we were friends. That will be all that it takes, and then we need to give ourselves a metaphorical hug.

That would be the pretext that we use to behave in this way, the excuse. But the reality is that we are eating outside of the hunger context; we are doing something that is mismatched with our needs; what we really need is some TLC, but we feed a body that does not need to be fed, and we gain weight as an outcome. Both outcomes are destructive and mutilating.

Strategy: Punish Those Who Threaten Rejection

We have an identity with food, which we closely guard, and then there is the identity we have outside of food, which we really do gain 'through' other people.

So when others challenge us, argue with us, or even just do not see us, we often find ourselves going to the food for our metaphorical hug, with the presenting thoughts, however, of wanting to get back at others.

Once again, the useful tool for this behaviour is food, and a 'heap load' of it, because the amount of food eaten is connected to the amount of frustration that we feel on such occasions.

In our younger days we could say that our strategies were survival mechanisms that helped us through the difficult times in life. However, they no longer work in that way now and are unhelpful and destructive to us: they reinforce our deep-seated belief that we are not good enough!

Food is a mechanism for diversion; it takes our mind off the situation, off ourselves, and enables us to 'do' something and feel better for doing it... except the diversion really does only last for a few short seconds.

Real Fact!

Food is on this planet to give our human bodies nutrition, and that is it.

We are so far removed from seeing food as just food. Look at how we have distorted that fact and the use of it.

So now that we are more aware of how we 'fit' into life – or, let's say, of how we are in life – and how food plays the part that it does for us, we now need to 'make good'.

Let us use the following analogy:

When we want to leave the house that has been our home for some time, we need to go and look for a new house. It is only when we find a new house that suits us, and one that we like, that we will move into it.

We must now create and understand our New House.

If we do not find that New House, we will always stay in the Old one.

We must find that new way of being, a different way of living, because without this we shall always have the weight issues, we shall always yo-yo diet, losing weight only to put it back on again, with possibly more. Most important, however, unless we find that new way, that we shall always be unhappy, and the dynamics of this Borderline Personality shall be extreme enough to hinder how we live, and shall be to the detriment of ourselves.

Our relationship with food reflects our relationship with life, reflects our thinking as a Borderline Personality. Our perspective as a Borderline Personality enables victim behaviour.

We will continue to see food as our answer to 'it all', and therefore continually gain weight, or continue with the life long-behaviour pattern of eating loads, and then restricting food, being fat, and then being thin, which in turn is the behaviour brought on by our extreme thinking.

"DO YOU KNOW WHAT KIND
OF FOOD IS THE MOST
NOURISHING?

THE BEST NOURISHMENT
COMES
FROM YOUR RELAXED
CALM
MIND.

IF YOU EAT FOOD BUT
HAVE A
TROUBLED MIND,
THE REULSTS WILL NOT
BE GOOD"

Chapter Six
VISUALISING A DIFFERENT WAY OF THINKING

What Does Our New House Need?

It would be easy for us to immediately say that we want the opposite of what we have in the Old House:

- Have the world as a kinder, fairer place

- Not worry so much about other people

- Do more for ourselves

- Like ourselves

- Have more fun in life

- Get thinner

- Stay thinner

- See food as just food…

… And it goes on. Once we get the hang of this, we will think of many more suggestions for how our New House could be.

We are now more aware of ourselves, of how we work, what drives us to do what we do, and the reasons we eat dysfunctionally. We have the knowledge that enables change.

However, it is in changing that we have the biggest task. Change to us is in itself the most difficult issue. To support change, there is something we can do which enables us to realise the emotional involvement in change.

115

See what you think to the following exercise.

Write down ten things that define your appearance and give you the identity you have chosen to have. For example, you

Always wear your watch on your left arm

Wear dark trousers with light-coloured tops

Have matching earrings

Wear matching underwear

Only ever wear trousers

Never wear make-up

Always wear mascara…
… And so on.

Once you have written these ten things down, you now need to *not* do one of them, or do one of them on following days for the week ahead. For example, if you wear your watch on your left wrist, then wear it on your right wrist for a day. If you wear dark bottoms with light tops, swap the colour co-ordination around so that you have light bottom and dark top.

Notice how each day feels.

What are your thoughts?

Do you think your changes stand out like 'sore thumbs' and yet no one else notices a thing?

See how you resist the change and how you like the identity you have with your appearance as it is.

In some ways, we could say that these are little and ineffective things to alter in order that we experience the full force of change. However, we might also realise that these changes impinge on the very identity we closely guard for ourselves.

This very effective exercise really does reflect how `stuck we are in our own rut, even to the point of how we dress!

Yet when it comes to losing weight, we do need to change quite a few things, do we not?

The reality of losing weight is that hopefully we will both desire and need to dress differently. Instead of wearing 'big baggies', we will want to wear clothes that fit us and show off our new-found figure. This puts us in touch with our sexuality, our femaleness. As females we have curves, we have breasts and a cleavage, we have hips, and in some cases those so-called 'child-bearing hips', which imply some quite distinctive curvatures. When we lose weight our body becomes redefined, and the desired effect of this is that we will be able to show these off more.

We definitely gain a different identity in society. However, as our sentence-completion exercise indicated to us, we move into a different and more 'sexual' place, and this can cause discomfort. Maybe it's not the case for all of us in regards to the discomfort, but there will be always some sort of emotional fall-out.

I worked with someone who lost a lot of weight. She travelled on the London bus service, and when she was fat, the conductor didn't look at her twice. However, when she lost all her weight, he started to offer her free travel. Although this lady was enjoying her new-found slimness, she was very angry that this meant she was offered free travel, and her comment to him was that she was still the same person, whatever size she might to be.

The desire to be thin, and the pressure from society telling us it is right to be thin, is very present for us all, but the change in ourselves and the changed response from other people, can sometimes become too difficult to tolerate, and the greater desire to return to that old identity and that old place often becomes too much... as we know. Hence the weight returns.

Now that we have brought to our awareness the discomfort we can experience let us, slowly move into our New House.

Whatever the change that we might be clear about wanting –for instance, being thinner, or having a life that is less of a struggle – all things different will be the result of a change in our thinking process. Let us look more closely, therefore, at how we think, what we think, and at our Jackanory Theme so that we can clearly understand what changes we need to make to live a calmer life.

We are now able to understand the type of personality we have – the Borderline Personality – and that is helpful to us because we can then see how it affects our relationship with food.

Let us also apply our view of others to our View of food:

We hold such strong beliefs that food is powerful– 'As long as it is not in the house, I'm alright!'

We idealize it. Our euphoric recall has us believe food can give us so much: make us feel good, get us feeling better, and make us feel warm, even when the food we crave is usually cold and hard, like crisps, chocolate, sweets, etc.

As with our experience with other people, the food that we eat ends up betraying us, and it definitely controls us, as we believe we cannot *not* eat it.

Our main trigger for eating food is feeling emotional.

We feel uncomfortable when we experience a greater intensity of emotions than we are used to, so we feed. Unfortunately, the food does not fill the void, or take away the discomfort, so our real experience of the food is that it lets us down; it creates a sense of rejection and abandonment because it does not give us the longed-for desire.

This is because food does not have the ability to fulfil emotions. In fact, food can never fulfil that side of us.

Interestingly enough, we can impose the view of others onto food in the same way that around food we can clearly see the view of ourselves being supported.

There is no doubt that we see and project a great deal onto everything and anything that is 'out there' that is outside of ourselves. This supports the Victim position we keep in life and it would be this thought that we really do need to challenge and change.

In the meantime, we always do things for other people, hoping that through this 'doing' we will have this emotional void of ours filled, that others will appreciate what we do, and that we will have our needs met in this way.

We are almost conditioned into saying 'yes' before thinking. Only after saying it do we start to wonder if it will be convenient for us, let alone manageable!

Now another exercise for us to see how we operate. Let's look at the type of things we do and the behaviours we are caught up in. Look at the following list and tick those that are appropriate.

1. Keep everything tidy, clean and tidy – to the point of getting up early and maybe vacuuming whilst the rest of the family are still in bed!

2. Demanding how things be done, having other people close to us doing things the way we do them, – if they are not able to do this then, not even allowing them to do it because we think there will be too much mayhem to deal with afterwards, resulting in us doing nearly everything, but hating it.

3. Work extra hours at our job, because we believe no one else can do the job right, and we like to think that we are absolutely the only person that can do it. We also like to be needed. This touches on megalomania, having an exaggerated idea of our own importance.

4. Do extra things to keep people happy.

5. Keep very busy.

6. Always say yes to others.

7. Do the housework every day before going to work, or maybe in our lunch break from work.

8. Have a set way of doing things in the house.

9. Always have to be the last person out of the house, or in bed at night… and any others you can think of.

10. Do all the fetching and taking of children or friends.

11. Shop for the family and maybe for elderly relatives.

12. Cancel arrangements for self because another member in the family has something to do at the same time.

13. Always washes up.

14. The only person to empty the dishwasher.

15. Pays the household bills

… And if you can think of others then add them to the list!

Now let us look at why we use these behaviours – why we do what we do. Once we look at this, we will begin to understand our belief systems. To understand these belief systems let us use this format: If I do … then …

So let's put some of the list we have just ticked into this format. The 'then' is about putting what we do in the context of other people, because of what we are driven to believe others think. Let us proceed.

If I keep everything tidy… then **others will think I am a good and organised person.**

If I demand how things be done… then **others will see how smoothly things run and how good I am at doing and organising everything.**

If I work extra hours and fill all the gaps in… then **others will see how good I am at my job, and I will always be kept on, promoted, etc.**

If I do things for other people to keep them happy… then **others will always want to be around me and see me as a happy person.**

If I keep myself busy… then **others will think that I am not lazy.**

If I always say yes… then **others will think I am polite.**

If I do the housework every day before I go to work… then **others will think I am efficient and a clean and tidy person.**

If I have a set way of doing things in the house, a routine… then **others will see that I do not forget and that I am meticulous.**

If I am the last person out of the house, or in bed at night… then **others will see me as caring.**

121

If I do all the fetching and taking of my children or friends…
then **others will see how much I love and take care of them.**

If I do all the shopping for the family and elderly relatives…
then **others will see I am a good housewife, daughter, etc.**

If I give up on my own arrangements… then **others will see me as being selfless – in other words, not selfish.**

If you have added more to the list, then see what comes to fruition, see what you think in the Jackanory place, because, of course, all the high-lighted parts of the sentences would be the 'Jackanory Theme, where we impose on others that which we think for ourselves. These are our own judgements!

We are also able to see that we are hugely influenced by what we think others think about us. In other words, by our own judgements!

According to Eric Berne's Transactional Analysis model, we see our Critical Parent with all the 'shoulds' and therefore act from the Adaptive Child. It is this part that drives us to always 'do' for others, in the hope that they will one day recognise that we have given so much and done so much that they say: 'Thanks!' …. And as we have worked out from a previous exercise, we are still waiting for that!

To continue, let's write down the feelings we avoid and apply the same format we used in the context of others:

If I share my feelings (this is something we do not do; this is something we avoid)… then **others will see me as vulnerable.**

Put this together and we have:

If I share my feelings… then **others will see me as vulnerable**

If I feel confident… then **others will think I am a show-off.**

If I feel angry… then others **will think I am rude, because I will shout uncontrollably.**

If I feel sad… then **others will think that I am depressing.**

If I feel irritated… then **others will be scared of being around me.**

To get in to the swing of this, add some more and see what you come up with.

Then there are things we avoid doing:

If I say what I think (again, this is not what we do)… then (what will others do) **others will shout back at me.**

Put this together:

If I say what I think…then **others will shout at me.**

If I want to do something of my own without agreement from others … then **others will leave me for good; they will abandon me.**

If I relax, and do nothing… then **others will think I am lazy.**

If I do things for myself … then **others will think I am selfish.**

If I am honest about my thoughts… then **others will judge me and not like me.**

The reason for doing this exercise is that if this book were to tell us to do something completely differently, we would either react from the Adaptive Child and do it, but only for a period of time, or we would become the Rebellious Child and reject it.

This way we will hopefully take on our own different thought process!

Be clear that nothing new is being brought into our 'world': all we are doing is using everything that we know but putting it altogether differently.

Let us now take three things that we do and three things that we avoid and change the thoughts that evolve from them, and we project onto others. This can be a little confusing, but practice enables a better grasp of this concept.

Three Things We Do:

> If I keep everything tidy… then **others will think I am a good and organised person.**

> If I keep myself busy… then **others will think I am conscientious.**

> If I do all the fetching and taking of my children or my friends… then **others will see how much I love and take care of them.**

Three Things We Avoid:

> If I share my feelings… then **others will see me as vulnerable.**

> If I feel and look confident… then **others will think I am a show-off.**

> If I do things for myself… then **others will think I am selfish.**

So use now the same 'doing' beginnings but with the 'avoid' endings:

If I keep everything tidy…

If I keep myself busy…

If I do all the fetching and the taking of my children or my friends…

… Then **others will see me as vulnerable.**

… Then **others will think I am a show-off.**

… Then **others will think I am selfish.**

So it might now look like this:

If I keep everything tidy… then **others will think I am a show-off.**

If I keep myself busy… then **others will think I am selfish.**

If I do all the fetching and the taking of my children and friends… then **others will see me as vulnerable.**

There is no set way of doing this, and I change things around in the way that I do for no real reason. Any match will work, although sometimes the understanding has to be searched for a little.

Then do this the other way, so putting the feelings we avoid with the endings of the things that we do:

If I share my feelings…

If I feel and look confident…

If I do things for myself…

... Then **others will think I am a good person.**

... Then **others will think I am conscientious.**

... Then **others will see how much I love them and take care of them.**

This now becomes:

If I share my feelings... then **others will see how much I love them and take care of them.**

If I feel and look confident.... then **others will think I am a good person.**

If I do things for myself.... then **others will think I am conscientious.**

So the new construct for the sentences looks like:

1. If I keep everything tidy, then others will think I am a show off.

2. If I keep myself busy, then others will think I am selfish.

3. If I do all the fetching and taking of my children and friends, then others will see me as weak.

4. If I share my feelings, then others will see how much I love them and take care of them.

5. If I feel and look confident, then others will think I am a good person.

6. If I do things for myself then others will think that I am conscientious.

It is hugely interesting for us to see how differently we can construct our sentences and match our thinking and our judgements differently.

Is our belief system distorted? Can we see the error of our thinking?

The analysis of the different constructs would be:

1. Keeping everything tidy, so tidy, can easily put others off. When our homes are kept so pristine what can happen is that other people come round and feel so intimidated by the neatness and the tidiness that they feel a failure because they cannot meet the same high standards. The consequent feelings of guilt can be enough to put them off wanting to come around again.

2. Keeping busy, we think, is a sign of goodness. However, whilst we are busy we do not have to get close to other people. We haven't got time to really relate to other people because we are too busy. We tend to live in our world of busyness, for example, when others come round to our homes uninvited we continue with our 'doing', which can appear very rude and selfish. We don't even have time to stop and talk and relate to others!

3. By fetching and taking everyone we can have the job done in the way that we like it. In fact, it is not the actual fetching and taking that is the issue here; this is part of the bigger picture of organising others and our environment. When we do it all, or at least so much of what needs to be done, we do so from a belief that we only understand and feel safe in the world if things are done our own way. This touches upon our vulnerability and is driven by a sense of weakness in us.

4. To feel comfortable enough to share our feelings with others means we trust both ourselves and others to be

safe. Consequently, we enable others to share in the same behaviour, and this is the way we get close relationships. We give permission to ourselves and to others to be real in a relationship, which often results in us being seen as caring, loving people.

5. Confidence is a strength, and with it we give ourselves more self value and respect. The respect we show, and share, is good. There is no over-compensating that has to go on, because confidence enables a quiet strength, with a great sense of self. We are therefore not overtly 'in other people's faces', as they say. This is a quality in people that others love to be around and be a part of.

6. Doing things for ourselves, not for other people but for ourselves, shows others that we are able to look after ourselves. Other people will see that we are not a burden or a responsibility to them, they will also see that if we are able to look after ourselves we are able to look after others if we choose to. There will be a sense of genuineness which will be seen as a relief. To be conscientious is generally viewed as being totally liberating for others and hugely OK.

In analysing the different couplings we can see there is a lot of truth in them, and this may even allow us the realisation that what we 'do', and how we are, does not work in our favour.

Our own judgments might have become distorted, for every sentence within the Jackanory Theme shows that we do not know how or what others think or do. **What we 'do' does not work for us. How we think is incorrect in so far as we have imposed our own thoughts on others. We must realise that we can do nothing else, we see the world in the way that we see it and we do not see it in the way that others do, so we cannot know how others feel or think**

This book has not 'fixed' anything. If we were to use other examples and put them in the same context – looking at what we do and then what we avoid in the context of others, changing the judgemental outcome part around – we would be able to see that maybe, just maybe, we are not seeing things and doing things that benefit us. We can jiggle all that we believe and get a different belief system going.

As Borderline Personality people we are very stuck in our ways, but we do not have to completely start afresh. All we have to do is jiggle our belief system
Conclusively, this work shows us that:

- All of the things that we do, and we do a lot, keeps people away from us.

- All the things and feelings we avoid also stops us from letting others get close to us.

Our relationship with food feeds into that isolation and that gap we create. It has become our constant friend and provider of our metaphorical hug. Yet the more beneficial and appropriate behaviour for us would be to reach out for support and warmth from others.

There is no doubt that other people do let us to do a lot for them This is not necessarily in their conscious awareness but comes automatically to them: it means that they do not have to look after and do for themselves. Anyone in their right mind would love to experience being looked after!

In doing a lot for others, we believe that they will like us more and want to be around us more. They will appreciate us and think all of those good things that we have just written about.

The reality is that others do not even notice half of the things that we do for them, it is not even apparent to them that we are working so hard to look after them.

Part of the reason for this is that by doing a lot of the periphery things for others, we take away their own ability to think for themselves and to look after themselves. Their awareness of their own needs has been violated by us doing for them all the time.

Above all – and this is the 'biggy' – we show ourselves no respect by doing so much for others which naturally introduces a lack of respect from others, as well as allowing them to behave helplessly. The other person in this relationship becomes quite impotent. He or she is eventually less able to do anything as they have not done for themselves for a long time, so they learn to rely on us.

This reliance breeds contempt as they then blame us when we have not been able to 'keep all those balls in the air', as there are now far too many for us to do whatever else it is they want us to do for them.

There is no benefit gained for either party: we have little respect for ourselves, and others show little respect for us and learn helplessness.

Through time, and this is cyclical, we begin to feel we are being used and we become tired and resentful; we give out a lot with nothing coming back to us, and we march forward to the 'blow up' scenario.

And within the 'blow up' we eat.

Our relationships are then based on what we can do for others; they are not necessarily based on like, love, respect, and emotional ties.

`Getting ready to move into the New House`

So the first step moving into the New House is that we let go of doing so much for others. Remember how our sentence construct can change to 'If we keep busy and do for others, then others will see us as megalomaniacs'.

If we really do not do all of these things for others, then they will have to start to pick up the pieces! They will begin to realise their own needs, possibly for the first time in a long time, and gain an understanding of what they need to fulfil those needs. Their awareness will be so much greater, which in time, will enable them to see outside of themselves.

So the journey begins!

It would very easy at this point to focus once more on the other person; in fact, we have already begun to do just that in this book with the paragraph just above.

What is the affect on us of letting go?

One huge leap in making this change in behaviour is for us to allow other people's behaviours to come into our lives. We are so nervous around allowing things to be done in another person's way, which drives us to do it all ourselves. As I once mooted to one of my groups, isn't life boring when you have everything your way, or at least done your way?

It's so ironic that we think so little of ourselves, and yet on the other hand believe beyond a shadow of a doubt that our way is the only way.

Yes, it will be different.

Yes, it will feel strange.

Yes it might not be done to the same standard, but can it not be 'good enough'.

If we do not 'do' so much, and if we relax our judgements, what do we gain? The world feels more relaxed, because we don't have quite so much to do.

We now have time to relate to others, because we can let go of some of the chores.

Other people can realise some of our own needs and therefore help us... we can start to share our lives a little.

How is the New House looking?

The important thing is that we communicate these changes; otherwise other people will not understand what is going on, and we will bring to fruition the beliefs we had in the exercise we did about needing to keep quiet and put up with things for fear of confrontation and abandonment.

So the second step in the New House is to find the true wants in our lives. The new construct and belief system would be 'If I do more of what I want, then others will see I am happier and will want to be with me more'.

In joining step one and step two, we will **want** to help others – when the time is right for us and the actual job or chore is one we can turn around into a like, or at worst, don't mind; there will be many an occasion in which we will want to help and do for another.

If we recollect our 'I Should' exercise, we see that it felt really different to put choice into it, so we could become clearer as to whether there was a real desire. It is about making the difference between what we want to do and what we think we 'should' do.

To help us make this shift from 'should' to 'want', maybe we can look at some guidelines:

- Do we have the energy to do it?

- Does it put us out a lot if we accept this job?

- Have we already done enough for today, and are we now tired?
- When do we relax today; maybe there is a gap in our day plan. We don't always have to be 'doing'!

- Do we want the outcome for what we are doing?

- Who are we really doing this for?

A lot of these answers will come from listening to our physical self and our emotional self.

We know how tired we feel, if it is convenient, and if it feels right for us to be doing whatever it is.

Look out for the guilt. Often we do things to avoid feeling guilty, but when we do this, we usually still feel fairly fed up about doing the task.

Two good indicators to run with are whether we have time on our side and whether we have real energy.

Taking a slight detour from the New House, for a moment, let us look at emotions briefly, and what our psychology has imposed on them, because with change will come a turmoil of emotion.

We tend to think that there are 'positive' and 'negative' emotions; society is always pushing us to look for the 'right' and the 'wrong', yet when it comes to emotions and ourselves as human beings, it is part of our humanness to feel the full range and to accept that this is absolutely OK.

Our bodies, our hearts, respond appropriately, and although an emotion such as sadness is uncomfortable… it really is OK.

There is absolutely no way that we can live without feeling sadness; if we were unable to experience such an emotion, then we would not know what it was like to feel real happiness.

We need to feel the full range to appreciate the full range, and we need to trust in ourselves, and to accept that when we do feel sad, or whatever it will be, it is appropriate.

Carl Rogers, a Person-Centred theorist (another school of therapy), suggests a 'fully functioning' person is able to accept the fact that we as people appropriately respond emotionally from across a broad spectrum of emotions to life.

Our Borderline Personality does find us vulnerable, and it is because of this that we have difficulty in allowing the full range of emotions; we believe the intensity of feeling will be overwhelming, and to some extent this may be true, because when we do anything for the first time the impact is so much greater.

Additionally, the problem most of us have is that 'forever' we have been given messages that have informed us not to trust the way we feel, messages that have taught us not to trust our own emotional responses. For example, when we fell over as a young child and scraped our knee, we felt pain and sadness, and yet the message was that the pain was not as bad as we thought – in fact, it was hardly there at all – and we were OK really, and should just get on with it.

The message left us confused. We were convinced we were in pain; our knee did hurt, and being told that this really was not the case caused us to question ourselves.

So it is hardly surprising that we do not allow ourselves to listen to our physical and emotional sides; we have never been given messages that suggest they tell us the truth.

Our journey, therefore, needs us to trust in our abilities and trust in the physical and physiological aspects of our humanness and to be unconditional to ourselves, because then we will accept ourselves.

For example:

When we are sad, accept that we are sad and allow ourselves to be able to sit quietly, maybe cry, and sometimes ask for a hug.

When we are angry, own it, and share it, but do not project it onto others.

To value ourselves means telling ourselves that what we feel is OK; allowing ourselves to respond appropriately to our emotions will introduce a completely different way of being; it will introduce a self-respect, which in turn will bring a response of respect from others.

This is what the Adult ego state in Transactional Analysis has... respect!

Now let us return to the point of 'want'. When we want to do things for other people, it will be because it is convenient for us, it will suit us, and we can be relaxed in doing it. It will then be our Adult, rather than our Adaptive Child, 'doing the doing'.

'Doing' whatever it is willingly, and with respect to ourselves and to others, will also result in more freedom too: there will be no 'tit for tat' condition; there will be honesty around doing it, because we want to.

This is a completely different dynamic than the 'doing' of an Adaptive child, who wants something in return, and has conditions around the apparently 'helpful' act.

Consequently, the response from the persons being helped will be different: they will be aware of our generosity and helpfulness, rather than possibly have contempt for us for knowing they can get us to 'do' anything.

When we do help others from choice they will feel special because we have chosen to help them; they will not feel as though they are one of many, which will produce a different type of relationship.

As we grow, with this feel-good factor produced by us doing more of what we want, we will feel less dependent on others giving us appreciation, because we will not need it as much; we will be giving to ourselves more.

If we look at the Borderline Personality, we will see the view of ourselves change:

- We start to feel MORE POWERFUL and more equal to others.

- We start to be more in control.

- We feel more relaxed and less abandoned and rejected.

In turn our view of others will be:

- They are not as powerful,

- They are less in control,

- They are less idealized,

and the world will not seem like such an unfair place.

Consequently, we will not have the internal tensions and stresses caused by subjugating our own needs, which we have needed to relieve through self-mutilation and self-destructive behaviour.

The urge to use food in this new house is much less!

"WE MUST EMPTY
OURSELVES
BEFORE WE ARE FIT TO
RECEIVE"

"THE JOURNEY OF A
THOUSAND
MILES BEGINS WITH ONE
STEP,
THE ROAD TO
ENLIGHTENMENT
BEGINS WITH EACH
MOMENT"

Chapter Seven

Behaviours from the Jackanory Theme

Our behaviours are always – always – a reflection of our thoughts, both in life and around food, so we must dig deep to realise the distortions we hold.

Our 'shoulds' can often be interpreted as 'wants', so we have to be careful when analysing the things we want, as they are easily confused.

A classic thought that many of us have is: 'I want to lose weight', and we then proceed to eat too much chocolate.

There is so much pressure in society for us to lose weight and be in that healthy weight range. Are we absolutely clear that we want to lose the weight? Or are we allowing others to tell us we 'should' lose weight.

When we want to lose weight, and yet eat in a way that does not enable us to have the outcome we want, we might benefit from looking into our thoughts. Is it that we do *not* want to lose weight, and that the 'want' in this thought is not genuine?

Or maybe we reflect the deeper thinking we have of not feeling 'good enough' about ourselves, in which case what we want we do not get, and we sabotage ourselves.

It is our subconscious thinking that needs to be realised and embraced here so that we can be honest with ourselves.

Our behaviour will always reflect our thinking; what we have difficulty in recognising sometimes is the level of thinking that our behaviour is reflecting.

So in the 'New House' we are looking into and letting go of our Jackanory Theme.

The Jackanory Theme is a reaction to believing that others do not speak the truth. We believe others do not speak the truth because, in essence, we do not speak the truth ourselves, and so we project this on to others. Examples we can easily identify with are:

- We say yes, but do not really mean it on many an occasion.

- We say we like something when we do not.

- We say we will 'happily' do something, knowing full well we do not have the time to do it, or even the inclination

- We say we are happy when we clearly are not.

In fact, we are not very honest people.

Because we are not honest with ourselves, and therefore with others, we cannot expect others to be honest and trustworthy with us. As the saying goes, 'A thief thinks everyone is a thief'. Of course this is the case, because we have only our own mind set to work from, our own yardstick, as previously mentioned.

This might be a harsh reality; we might find this a little too brutal to take, or to accept. However, this is the breeding ground for a lot of our distress, and definitely the cause of our Jackanory Theme. If we said what we truly meant, but in a way that we own how we see and feel the scenario then we would be able to allow others to say what they truly mean and take exactly what they say as 'gospel'!

In this honest place we would also be able to put our needs to the front of the queue.

This change would be so profoundly life-changing, because then our strategy of subjugating our own needs', would not be in place, and we would then embrace our own needs. To embrace our own needs would mean we would not be living so near the 'end of the fuse', and then if people did not say hello, for instance, we would be able to tolerate such an oversight.

In a slightly different way, but looking again at the New House, here are some of our own needs:

- Doing more of what we enjoy

- Letting go of the responsibility of making other people happy – in other words knowing, 'I'm OK, you're OK'.

- Being able to say no.

So the fourth step in the New House is saying the word 'no'.

This is an incredibly troublesome word. This two-letter word is so often the most difficult word for us to say because the underlying belief is: 'If I say no then… others will think I'm selfish.' Other thoughts with this could be:

- 'If I say no, then … others will value the times I say yes.

- 'If I say no, then … others will know they are special when I say yes.

- 'If I say no, then… others will respect me and my limitations.

Without 'no' the word, 'yes' has no real meaning.

Once again it is about finding balance, that middle ground. We do not want not to help others, but we do need to learn to help only when it fits in with our already demanding life. It is about helping when it feels right to, helping when we have the time, and when we want to do whatever it is.

We need to recognise that we have our own wants. We like, and we do not like, and we do not have to be the Victim or the Martyr in the Drama Triangle.

When we recognise this, the Nurturing Parent is more present, accepting us for who we are, allowing us our likes and our 'dislikes, embracing the fact that we want to do some things and not others.

Our nurturing side accepts our limitations as humans beings, accepts that we get tired, that we are not being lazy, that we will not always help, and that that does not make us selfish.

Sometimes we make choices that will benefit us, and sometimes we do not; this does not make us bad or good – it is just as it is!

The word 'infallible' – never wrong, never failing – is sometimes applied to the human way of being, which suggests that we as humans are not necessarily wrong or failing.

When a judgement is made about something we do as being wrong or failing it will derive from the agenda of the person that makes the judgement. That person is not agreeing with what we do, it is not final however that this is the case. We are all individuals who do what we do for the reasons we have and although our individuality can be perceived or / and judged by others it does not mean they are right and we are wrong.

We as beings are not perfect, and nor do we really want to be as in all honesty life would be so totally boring if this were the case.

When we can accept the 'warts' we have, and accept that we do what we do for the reasons we have in the moment that we do it, we will at last accept ourselves, our very selves. We will be able to sit comfortably with our dislikes and likes, even share them with others, and have fun with who we are without mocking ourselves.

As we read this, hopefully we are able to find a greater sense of calm and to let go of the ever-present judgements made by our Critical Parent.

Are we now feeling a little relaxed? Do we feel a little less stressed? Are we beginning to accept who we are … just a little? This would be number five in our New House: to accept ourselves for who we are.

Our New House will need different strategies too. Subjugating our own needs has already been looked into. So when looking at the other strategies, such as relieving tension through self-mutilation and self-destructive behaviour, we find that the amount of tension present will decrease if we just allow ourselves to be who we are.

When there is a greater sense of calmness, the stress that we hold on to – and to such an acute degree – is diluted, so when anything extra occurs – and we know it always does – we have more reserve to draw from; we are not overflowing from life to start off with, so we are able to manage those extras a whole lot better.

The last strategy, punishing those who threaten rejection, would turn into being able to let go of those others. We would set the boundaries between us and others. Doing more of what we want and having distance between ourselves and others will lessen greatly the need to 'punish' them, or even 'take on' what others think. That 'cutting our nose to spite our face' type of behaviour will be replaced by behaviour that benefits us. We will be giving enough back to ourselves, so the affect of others on us will not be so huge; we will not 'catastrophise' our reactions or emotions.

So the sixth step in the New House is promoting the middle ground.

We know more of who we are; we have our own wants and desires; we accept that we are not everything to everyone and that we are a mixture of many things. For example, we might think we are shy; we become consumed by that belief and hate ourselves for being this way.

However, in reality we are probably only shy on certain occasions, occasions when it is perfectly reasonable for us to be shy – for instance, when we do not know anyone.

Let us look at other examples where we might realise the middle ground:

- **Confidence**

  - When it comes to our children's welfare, we are able to stand up for them and our beliefs.

  - As a woman, going up to the bar in a pub where there are many men can make us feel unconfident. This would be perfectly normal, as sometimes men in a group can be experienced in a very over-powering way. If the bar had only women we would feel very different.

  - When we are at home and we want something to happen in the home in the way we want it to happen, we feel confident that we are right in wanting this.

  - When it is the end of the week, and the budget is tight, we do not feel confident about going into an expensive shop and even just looking around. When we are feeling a bit more flush we have the financial back-up to go into that shop.

In other words, we are experiencing different levels of confidence around different things in life. So for us to believe that we are 'absolute' and have no confidence all the time would be distorted.

It is so easy for us to go to that extreme place again and get caught up with a wholeness of our emotions, and yet the reality is that we feel so much in one day and our reactions emotionally to all the things that we experience are an assortment of feelings.

We need to be aware of the different ways we feel through the course of a day, and to know that our feelings enable us to understand that certain things are OK for us and that other things are not OK for us. Our feelings give us the opportunity to keep ourselves safe.

Early in the book we learnt about how the brain works. We looked at how dopamine – the fight or flight chemical –works for us. We also read of how our emotions enable us to be humans: when happy we feel relaxed and want to laugh; when scared we want to withdraw and keep quiet. These are all reactions to our emotions and they keep us safe.

Often when I meet with ladies on a weekly basis and enquire as to how they are they will reply in such a way that suggests the whole week has either been 'bad' or 'good'. I respond by asking how a whole seven days – many, many hours – can be summarised into one of two available words. It seems to omit so much living, yet this is often the way we view the world and our experience of it.

So the seventh step in the New House is to live in the moment, experience it, and not to keep moving away from it by thinking about the future and summing whole chunks of life into one aspect.

It is often the case that we constantly look forward to something; we have a holiday, come home, and then book the next one so that we have that anchorage in life, to look forward to something. We fill our diaries up with dates of meetings with friends; God forbid that we have any time in which we do nothing.

Even our society reinforces this: as soon as Christmas is over and New Year takes us into January 1st, the shops are selling Easter Eggs. Valentines cards come out the beginning of February, and so it goes on. Only when it proves to be totally crazy do the shops let go of having something important to look forward to. Let it not be overlooked that Christmas appears to come out in August now – with each year the introduction of the festive time seems earlier.

Where has living in the moment for the moment gone?

We all enjoy our holidays so very much? How is that? We relax. We do not really 'do' anything. We take each moment for what it is and what it can give us, because we want to squeeze everything into our precious days away from home. We allow others to look after us a little. We laugh more

We are happy more often. We could think of many other changes that holidays seem to allow of us. Let us have more of this: if we look after this moment, then the next moment will look after itself.

When we begin to involve ourselves honestly as emotional beings, it does not mean that we fall to pieces in the middle of the floor. It means we begin to allow ourselves to have reactions that include feelings as well as thoughts, and it results in us experiencing life fully and in us managing life fully. We are allowing ourselves to become full human beings, with wishes, wants, and emotions.

Looking again at our Borderline Personality and our view of others, our perception is of others being powerful, ideal, as well as controlling, rejecting, and abandoning; we look to others for that sense of fulfilment and happiness and yet they are never able to give enough and we are not in the right place to receive it.

What we have done is project onto others our own abandonment of self. We have rejected who we are, betrayed ourselves and our humanity. How many of us do have a full-length mirror in our homes? I am sure not many. This represents how we have 'cut off' our bodies from our heads, how we have disowned our bodies.

We do not want to own our bodies; we never really touch our bodies; we probably do not even moisturise our bodies; we do not see them, we just cover them up; we mutilate them with our overeating; we destroy them by overeating, and by giving them food when they are not ready for it.

In the 'New House we do not do this to the degree or with the frequency we have in the past. There will be times when life gives us an extreme experience, such as the loss of a loved one, moving house, separating, or some other major change for which over-eating will seem to be the appropriate remedy, but this will be time limited and therefore is not as abusive.

In the New House we now need to begin to embrace our bodies, our whole selves. Let us care for them and touch them; let us comfort them in that nurturing way, and let us put a stop to the over-use, the vast demands, we put on them.

Once we connect with ourselves in full, we become aware of – and will be in tune with – our body's real needs, and then be aware of the body's state of fullness. Our body, which holds our feelings in the solar plexus, near our stomachs, will then be able to give us our awareness and enable us to begin to become more fully-functioning beings.

If we were to take the exercise we completed in Chapter Four and do it from the New House, it would go like this:

1. Once again choose a situation, preferably the same type as before so that you are able to see a difference in yourself:

2. How would we like to be, and for the situation to be?

- In this relationship, we want our own needs to be as important as the other person's. We do not need to put other people's wants before our own.

- We want to be embraced by the other person within this relationship as we embrace them, and to be sharing a common interest in each other.

Being seen as having confidence, more respect for ourselves, occurs in us when we initially lose our weight. However, we now need to make sure that this goes deeper than the skin, than the visual impact we create. We want to take this into our being.)

3. If the situation were like this how would we feel?

We would be looking for that feeling of calmness that
comes from being equally present in the relationship. We
would also feel happy, empowered and grounded in our
relationship.

4. How would we see ourselves if the situation were like this?

I am...   (Equal, empowered, and OK, and *good enough*.)

5. How would we see the other person?

Others are... (Just normal; they are there, and they are fine,
but they are not anyone to look up to; they are off the
pedestal that we had put them on, and they are 'just'
people.)

A good illustration of the need to look after ourselves first and
foremost is seen when we watch the flight stewardesses go through the
safety presentation in an aeroplane. They state that if the oxygen masks
are needed, parents *must* put them on themselves *first*, and only then
place the masks over our children's faces – a wonderful example of the
parents having to look after themselves first, because if they do not
then they will not be able to look after their children.

This is so true; if we do not look after ourselves first, then we
will not be able to look after, and do for, others. We have to look after
ourselves first; there is no one else able to do this in the exact way we
need to be looked after, because no one else knows us the way we do.

Returning to the exercise:

6. The world is... (Kinder now, more friendly, and more
accepting, less lonely; we have more companionship; it
feels less hostile, and warmer.) Now let us look at the new
underlying beliefs.

- If we say no, then… we are needing to say no because we either do not want to say yes, or due to logistics feel we are unable to say yes.

If others do not like hearing us say no, then it will be because of their own 'stuff' in life. Let's face it: if any of us want someone else to do something for us, we are naturally disappointed when they do not do it, but, hey, life is like that, and we are still OK.

- If we sit down, then… we are tired, and deserve to sit down, and we are not lazy for doing so.

- If we do not always do things, and are therefore not always busy, then… we are realising our own limitations, and know that we want to rest, and others can do what they like with that.

- If we say something that leads to someone being upset, then… we can explain that this was not our intention, and we are saddened by the reaction this has caused, and ask if they are OK.

- We do not need to take full responsibility for their sadness, as we know it was not our intention to produce this feeling.

- If we are sad, then… we have experienced something that has caused us to feel sad; others do not have to *do* anything to help us, as being sad is OK; it is what we do as humans.

- If we feel any sort of emotion, then… we are reacting appropriately to the situation and will benefit from looking after ourselves with those feelings. Others can choose to stay around if they wish to.

There are so many other – and changed – thoughts we can have in this New House of ours. The fundamental difference is that we let go of feeling responsible for other's welfare and stand fast with our own.

For us to be able to bring this New House to fruition we have to come away from our 'telepathic' place in the world and gain what Marsha Lineham calls 'interpersonal skills', otherwise known as the art of communication.

It has always been our way to keep quiet, to wait for that mythical happy life, and to live in the hope of things turning out as we want them to.

How do we say what we think and overcome the feeling of fear that we have around putting our thoughts, putting ourselves, and our needs forward, without fearing – and possibly experiencing – confrontation? I wonder if by being 'present' and bringing ourselves into a relationship or discussion we have to be confrontational, we can be firm and assured but we do not have to be hostile.

As long as we do not 'point the finger' at the other person and can communicate ourselves and our presence in a way that we own all said then this will not be confronting and shall be heard by the other person and responded to in a way that is mutually friendly and accepting.

To soften the anxiety around being present we can look into some statements that we can make *before* we say what we really want to say. Let us think of a few:

- 'I'm finding this difficult to say, so please do not shout.'

- 'I wonder if it will feel comfortable for you to hear this; I do not want to offend you and yet I do want to say....'

- 'This is hard for me to say, and yet I do need to say this.'

- ' I really do not want to upset you, and yet I would like to say....'

149

- 'I need to say something.'

- 'This is difficult to say, so I would appreciate you just hearing me out.'

- 'I really just do not want to do (fill in), and at the same time I hear that you want to, and that is OK in the same way as I do not want to'

There is also a statement that saves us every time if we are not sure of what we are feeling or thinking:

'I'll have to get back to you about that I'm not sure.'

These statements reflect the honesty we have been reading about in this book; they allow us to be present in relationships even if we are not sure about how we feel in that equally balanced place, or know how we want to be. They share the uncertainty that the human species does experience in life.

They also let us open ourselves up to others; they share us, which can be viewed as quite daunting. However, we are 'just' speaking the words that describe how we feel, we are not necessarily sharing the experience of them. They give us our way into communication with others.

What has this got to do with anything? What are we doing with all of this? What bearing does this have on food, my relationship with it, and my weight?

Let us reiterate that our relationship with food merely reflects our relationship with ourselves and with others.

Food enables behaviour rooted in the Borderline Personality, but also found rooted in the Rebellious Child, the Adaptive Child, the Critical Parent, and the Victim (which funnily enough, I have placed last... in the position of a victim).

Depending at which level we analyse the thoughts, we can be

found to behave deceitfully and sneakily in our 'Rebellious Child', or finish eating the plate of food as an Adaptive Child, and because we listen to our Critical Parent.

As Borderline Personalities, we have strategies that support our silence and keep us invisible. However, when we choose to communicate, awkwardly at first, we position people the same as us; we have equal importance, which could be seen as having more confidence, having more self–respect, and being able to walk tall: the trees are a wonderful green; we notice the world we live in, for its colours and its openness; let us feel happy with this place and with how we stand.

We believe in ourselves; we *are* OK; we are not 'right' and we are not 'wrong'; we are who we are, and for the reasons we have, we do what we do. We care about ourselves.

Then, and only then, do we not need the metaphorical hug. We do not need to harm ourselves; we do not need to destroy ourselves; we do not need to punish others. We can live less stressfully and be more relaxed.

Our 'New House' finds us talking, finds us having the interpersonal skills that enable us to fulfil our needs so that we can receive the proper 'hugs' that we want and not the metaphorical hugs we gather through food.

"IN THE BEGINNERS MIND
THERE
ARE MANY POSSIBILITIES,
BUT IN THE EXPERTS
MIND
THERE ARE FEW"

"GO BEYOND THE
THOUGHT OF WHAT"

"STRIVE TO BE AT PEACE
WITH
YOURSELF"

Chapter Eight

BEING REAL

Our 'New House' is beginning to have a different feel about it.

- We are getting more of our own needs met, because we are tentatively putting our voice forward and saying things into the open.

- We are sharing our own perspective on life and our views about things, which engages us in learning other people's views on life. This is very significant for us, as it is the catalyst for us to come out of our rut and fill it with other aspects, ideas, angles, and understandings. People will automatically act differently when we act different with them:

- We experience sharing, conversing, an exchange of ideas, and not confrontation.

- We experience our lives in the moment, rather than thinking about the next thing all the time. This is so very important when it comes to our eating, because when we are in the moment we are far more accountable to ourselves for the food choices we make, rather then excuse them with an insignificant long-term solution that never comes to fruition.

- We are not destroying ourselves with food anywhere near as much, because we are experiencing life; we are more satisfied with and stimulated by it and ourselves. So food becomes 'lame' for us.

- We are not mutilating ourselves with food, because we are used to engaging in what we want more, and we want to let go of the weight and keep it off. We want to eat the food types that 'bide' us well.

- Others are not affecting us as much, because we are more concerned with ourselves, and because it does not have to be an, either-or situation, this will not be to the detriment of others.

This is sounding and feeling so much better for us; we are so much more alive in this 'New House, and more stimulated by the broader options, and by the difference we can now see in our lives.

To round this off, let us look at the Transactional Analysis theory of 'strokes.'

The concept of strokes is important because through it we can eventually engage in really accepting the nice things that can be said to us. When this occurs, we are more fully functioning human beings. To illustrate this, I give you a passage from a book called *The Velveteen Rabbit,* written by Margery Williams:

'… What is REAL?' asked the Rabbit one day, when they were lying side by side near the nursery fender, before Nana came to tidy the room. 'Does it mean having things that buzz inside you and a stick-out handle?"

'REAL isn't how you are made,' said the Skin Horse, 'It's a thing that happens to you. When a child loves you for a long, long time, not just to play with but REALLY loves you, then you become REAL.'

'Does it hurt?' asked the Rabbit.

'Sometimes,' said the Skin Horse. For he was always truthful, 'When you are REAL you don't mind being hurt,'

'Does it happen all at once, like being wound up,' he asked, 'or bit by bit?'

'It doesn't happen all at once,' said the Skin Horse.

'You become. It takes a long time. That's why it doesn't often happen to people who break easily, or have sharp edges, or who have to be carefully kept. Generally by the time you are REAL, most of your hair has been loved off, and your eyes drop out, and you get loose in the joints and very shabby.

But these things don't matter at all, because once you are REAL you can't be ugly, except to people who don't understand.'

'I suppose you are REAL?' said the Rabbit, and then he wished he had not said it, for he thought the Skin Horse might be sensitive.

But the Skin Horse only smiled.`

To be real for ourselves is probably one of the hardest things we can do. It would be very easy for us to fall into the, `same old` thinking that for us to be real would depend on how others are, but when we truly believe we are real, we are able to give ourselves enough so that other peoples input is not as important to us as it was before.

Sure, it is great to receive these strokes… depending on the type they are. But we have to give them to ourselves first in order to truly take them from others. Otherwise, they will bounce off us.

So let us look at the types of 'strokes. There are strokes that can be labelled 'warm fuzzies'. The reason I offer you this alternative label is because I believe we are immediately able to feel a sense of warmth from them. I know I certainly want to hug myself when I think about these strokes.

Understandably, these are the only strokes we really like and want. When we look at the Borderline Personality, it is these strokes that we yearn to get from other people, and yet think we never do.

There are other strokes that we are unfortunately far more familiar with and comfortable in receiving.

So what are strokes? Well, they are defined as a 'unit of recognition'.

We are now aware that because of the Borderline Personality we like to be hugely recognised for what we do; that is why we work so hard. However, we never seem to get enough of these 'warm fuzzies', and as a result of this we do always feel deprived.

The challenging question is whether we really are clear about their absence, or whether we just find it so difficult to take them when they are offered.

There are different kinds of strokes. Unfortunately, because of the type of personality we are, we have experienced certain types only too often. We can classify three kinds:

- Verbal and non-verbal

- Positive and negative

- Conditional and unconditional.

Although we could easily rush through them, let us take time to really understand how these work.

Verbal and Non-verbal Strokes

Scenario One

We find ourselves walking in the park with our pet dog; our dog meets another and the owner gives us a smile.

This would be seen as a non-verbal stroke being offered to us.

Without too much ado, we then respond, and possibly smile, or even say hello, which would then be considered a verbal stroke.

So far so good!

Scenario Two

We find ourselves in the park again, walking our dog, and the owner of the other dog looks at us and frowns.

Naturally, we would see this as a negative non-verbal stroke.

Our response would most probably be one of looking away, or hurrying off, both being negative non-verbal strokes because we are responding to an already-set negative environment.

It is not often that we would find ourselves responding in a non-reflective way; we will usually become drawn into the set tone of the interaction. This embraces the view of others that we have, in so far as we 'give others the power to initiate the tone; we wait for them to offer recognition to us, otherwise we would just walk on.

It could even be said that the frown we receive would not necessarily surprise us, as we view others to be rejecting, abandoning and controlling.

The Scenario Two experience can easily leave us feeling rather fed up, bewildered as to why another person would want to frown at us, but also on the sub-conscious level believing we are used to such responses and that this is all very normal.

Positive and Negative Strokes

Scenario Three

Again taking our beloved Poochie for a walk, we see another dog owner, with a cute dog, and the dogs meet. We both see how our dogs are getting along, and the other person might say, with a smile on her face, 'They look as though they have known each other for years.' We would then respond in that equally delightful way by saying, 'It is nice to see them getting on.'

We can easily see how these are both positive verbal strokes.

Let us note that both parties involved were also able to receive these strokes in a pleasurable way.

Scenario Four

Again, we are walking our dog. The owner of another dog shouts at us when the dogs get together, although the dogs are fine. 'Get your stupid dog away from mine!'

Both of us would no doubt find this interaction, this form of recognition, somewhat loud and confrontational; it would be painful for us to experience.

Let us note, however, that although we can imagine wanting to seek out only positive strokes, in reality we can often find ourselves working on the different principle that any stroke (recognition) is better than no stroke at all.

To back this theory, if we look at people in sale, during their training there will always be an emphasis on getting some type of reaction. An agreement is great and is what they look for; an objection will give them something to work on, even though it is a negative reaction – a negative stroke – they have a reaction – recognition – to work with.

When people are indifferent, and therefore show little expression, share only apathy, and have no conviction either way, then the salesperson will almost always fail to get a business agreement: there is nothing reflected, nothing to react to, and nothing to work with.

When we do not experience any recognition at all we naturally wither, and that is why even negative strokes then become important to us.

Conditional and Unconditional Strokes

A conditional stroke relates to what we do. Hopefully, this will immediately ring alarm bells as we are renowned for doing... aren't we? In other words, this type of stroke will only be given on the basis of doing something for someone else, of being that 'Adaptive Child'.

An unconditional stroke relates to who we are.

Scenario Five

We are out walking with our dog, and the other dog owner says, 'The dogs are getting on so well, and your dog seems so well–behaved. You have trained your dog well – that must be why the dogs appear to be happy'.

This is both a positive and a conditional stroke.

We will possibly feel uncomfortable with this stroke because we do find it difficult to acknowledge and accept that what we do warrants praise and appreciation. Yet, on the other hand, this is so what we crave.

We, hopefully, respond in a way that minimises the suggestion we have done something good, but still acknowledges we have done something useful if nothing else:

'Yes he is a good dog. I haven't had to train him much, and they do look very happy together, don't they?'

Scenario Six

The dogs stop to sniff each other, and this brings a halt to our walking. The other person smiles and says, ' It's great to see you again. I like meeting you when we are out.'

As we are not being noted for anything we do, just for being who we are, this is an unconditional stroke.

The possible conflict with these two types of strokes is that we might receive them in an uncomfortable way, because we are not used to being given any positive recognition.

We are the product of our experiences, and almost none of us in early childhood received positive strokes, the 'warm fuzzies', we both needed and wanted. So we figured out ways to get the negative ones. Painful as they were, in our early days they were preferred, as opposed to getting nothing at all. Food fits in beautifully here as it is our negative stroke, the difficulty that can arise for us sometimes is that when we stop the eating and therefore stop giving ourselves the negative stroke we have a huge gap, we have nothing else to give ourselves we have that place of indifference which is really quite uncomfortable. Now that we are grown up, and have experienced many years of finding comfort in the negative strokes, we are really only comfortable with those types. So when we are given the positive, either conditional or unconditional, they give us that squirmy feeling.

As for the positive recognition for who we are, we quickly skim over these!

Many people (and our 'Critical Parent') will often give a positive stroke, but with a sting to it, and if they do not add the sting, we most probably will. By a sting I mean comments shown in the following examples:

- That's a lovely coat... did you buy it at the second-hand shop?

- Your home is lovely... for the age it is.

- I like your top… was it £5 from the market?

Hopefully, we can recognise that if they left the stroke as 'I like your top', we would more often than not end it with 'What this old thing? I got it from a cheap market stall' and put the sting on ourselves.

The discomfort is overwhelming for us when we receive these positive strokes, and yet they are the strokes we yearn for. Knowing this helps us to recognise the difference between our familiar comfort zone and the zone that is nurturing for us – they feel worlds apart.

The man behind Transactional Analysis, Eric Berne, calls this 'marshmallow throwing'. The positive stroke is given, and then taken away with a somewhat negative comment, which indicates insincerity in the first part of the remark.

We are very aware of 'marshmallow throwing', because it is the latter part of the remark that stays with us. We hear the criticism more then anything else because we think we deserve it.

If we are given a stroke that we are not used to, or does not fit in with our familiar and preferred type of stroke, we are likely to ignore it, or even belittle it.

This is known as 'filtering out' the stroke.

As Borderline Personalities with a belief that we are not good enough, and powerless around others, we find it very difficult to receive positive strokes that are forthcoming to us, so we, filter them out by either laughing them off or awkwardly saying 'thanks'.

When we are alone with ourselves we will also find it extremely difficult to remember, accept, or recognise that we have ever been given any positive strokes, which exacerbates that 'poor me' place, and the 'Victim' in us, as well as the martyr.

When we look at strokes on the whole, we can recognise that we frequently offer positive strokes. For instance:

- ' I like your trousers.'

- ' Gosh, you look great.'

- ' You are so kind.'

- ' You're so good at your job.'

… And we go on, and we go on, and we go on.

The reason for the persistent offering of positive strokes is our underlying hope that one day we will get some back.

When it comes to receiving strokes, however, we feel more comfortable with the negative types because we are able to identify with them, as they reflect our belief systems about ourselves. Some examples would be:

- 'I only deserve to struggle.'

- 'I look horrid most of the time, especially when I am fat.'

- 'No one likes me, 'cause I'm not a nice person.'

- 'I need to work really hard and find things difficult so that I can be appreciated'

… And so on, and so on, and so on.

The survival mechanisms we have created for ourselves involves keeping others out, distant enough that we do not get hurt, as we have been in the past.

Life really can feel very unsafe and scary at times. We often feel it is not safe enough to let positive, unconditional strokes in because of the pain we have experienced. So we keep that stroke filter really tight, and often disallow positive strokes that are offered. Unfortunately, this deprives us of the strokes that we could receive quite safely as grown-ups.

It is necessary that we have more of these positive strokes, both conditional and unconditional, in our New House. More pats on the back for ourselves are very necessary, as we know without them we find ourselves withdrawn and depressed.

It is interesting to look back into the generations before us and make ourselves aware of the messages around strokes and self--appreciation. If we talked to our elders it became quite apparent that to be proud of ourselves, or pleased with how we looked, was being 'big-headed'! If we overtly shared and showed our own pleasure in something we had done or in how we looked there was a strong judgment made: this was 'arrogant', 'showing off', even 'selfish' – and all of them meant 'not acceptable'. For the most part, we should always think that we must have more to do, or that we could do better, with the underlying message being that we can never do well enough.

Claude Steiner believes that as children we are all indoctrinated by the generation before us with five restrictive rules about strokes.

1. Don't give strokes when you have them to give.

2. Don't ask for strokes when you need them.

3. Don't accept strokes if you want them.

4. Don't reject strokes when you don't want them.

5. Don't give yourself strokes.

Steiner calls this the 'Stroke Economy'.

The previous generation, due to their own background, have limited the amount of strokes they've given us. As in the world of economy, when the demand is high but the supply is low, then the value is precious. So when we are trained into the idea that there are a limited amount of strokes, our parents can extract a high value from them. More importantly the provider of these strokes also becomes very important, and so through this dynamic parents could and can gain a sense of control over us.

Consequently, we were taught that strokes were in short supply, and as children we focussed very much on our parents being the only ones that were able to give them, so they became the 'stroke monopolists'.

Putting this together, the parents become the stroke monopolists in the stroke economy of low supply but high demand, and strokes then have precious value. We are talking about positive strokes. However, let us not forget that we do want strokes of any kind because they are signs of recognition, and without them we believe deep down that we would not exist.

So our relationship with our parents becomes based on what we can do for them, in order that we can gain the conditional stroke. The more we help them, the more we might possibly get a few positive conditional strokes.

As we become older, we tend to project that position of stroke monopolists onto others, as we see ourselves doing a lot for others, and looking after them so that they might offer the positive conditional strokes. However, by this stage we are so brain-washed' into thinking that we are only allowed a very few positive conditional strokes that we are unable to recognise the ones over and above the 'normal' amount that do come our way.

So in our New House we could implement a thinking that allows us a limitless supply of strokes:

- We can give a stroke whenever we want.

- It doesn't matter how many strokes we give out.

- Strokes will never run out.

- When we want a stroke we can ask for one.

- When we are given a stroke we can freely accept it.

- If we do not like a stroke, then we can openly reject it.

- We can enjoy giving ourselves strokes.

There is a myth about stroking that almost all of us are taught: strokes that we have to ask for are worthless!

The reality is that if we want a stroke, and we ask for it, then it is the equal in worth of one we receive unsuspectingly. Think of how we ask for things for our birthdays or for Christmas, and when we get them it feels great, because we have been heard. Strokes are really no different.

If we connect this to the Borderline Personality, we can see that we have suffered hugely from the deprivation of those 'warm fuzzies'. Thinking that we are not 'good enough' and therefore driving ourselves to 'do' so much in the hope that we can be given some strokes, yet ironically, filtering them out, even when we are given some. As if we were children again, we look to others to have the power and the control, to give us that recognition, yet we are really only experiencing that rejection, abandonment and betrayal.

To begin the process of change, to enter that doorway of the New House, we really do need to recognise that we can ask for positive strokes, but possibly more importantly, let us learn from within that we can give ourselves positive conditional and unconditional strokes.

There is a poem by Jenny Joseph called "Warning when I am an old woman" that encapsulates exactly the difference between letting go of the 'shoulds' and the Borderline Personality in its extreme. It is about allowing ourselves, accepting ourselves, accepting our individuality and our humanness. With a touch of humour she writes about a woman whom when old will wear purple and let go of all the `properness` of life; "and I shall spend my pension on Brandy and Summer gloves". She gives wonderful examples of the many different ways we can loosen up with ourselves; "and run my stick along public railings".

Then makes the comparison of how so many of us seem to think we `should` live; "But now we must have clothes that keep us dry" immediately we sense the sensible side of life come through, "We must have friends to dinner and read the newspaper" almost inferring the boredom of middle ageness

This illustrates beautifully how we are somewhat constrained by the received order of acceptability in society and how we are compelled to stay within the parameters of presumed normalness. The Critical parent holding us back in a restrained and constrained manner.

Yet there is another side to us. We are almost screaming out to be that Rebellious Child who stands in the rain and throws caution to the wind.

It is only when we are able to give ourselves enough positive strokes that we shall wear purple and feel calm and OK about doing so.

Our new house has a mixture of purple and Adaptive Child!

"WHEN WE CAN
CONTROL OUR
THOUGHTS
WE CAN CONTROL THE
MANIFESTATIONS OF
OUR
THOUGHTS"

Chapter Nine

PUTTING IT ALL TOGETHER

So How Does This Affect Us with Food and with Our Eating?

We have now read and learnt so much about who we are and how we function. We find that there is theory that explains our behaviour patterns, and we realise that our eating is as a result of who we are and a reflection of how we relate to people and the world.

It has been nonsense, therefore, to believe that we can tackle the food issues in isolation, by being on a diet, without embracing the deeper work of our fundamental relationships in life.

When the essence of our outlook on life and our behaviour in life is changed, so too shall our food behaviours, eating behaviours, and weight issues alter.

In summary, let us attempt to put all the strands together.

Core Issues

1. Borderline Personality

- We are powerless, needy and not good enough.

- Others are in control, powerful and idealized.

- We eat because we overlook our own needs.

- We are so stressed that we need to self-destruct and self-mutilate.

- We always believe that others are going to leave us and live with the fear of that abandonment.

So we hardly ever say what we think, and what we feel, and the word 'no.

Other people are so much more important.

2. We are Victims

'Other people are so lucky because they do not have the weight problems we have!'

3. Critical Parent, Adaptive Child, and Rebellious Child

There are too many 'shoulds' and not enough 'wants' in our lives. We are unable to prioritise our own needs in the midst of these ego states.

Middle Issues

1. Beliefs that we need others

If other people do not respond in the way we want, or see fit to respond, then we take it personally and feel rejected.

2. Jackanory Theme

We always impose on others our own way of thinking and imagine such elaborate stories to scenarios.

Surface Issues

1. We eat out of habitual behaviour

- Because we come home from work.

- Because we 'feel' more than we usually 'feel'.

- Because something has not gone right and we are stressed by it.

- Because we are bored.

- Because at that time…of the day…we eat.

- Because we are scared of the thought that we might not be able to sustain feelings of hunger.

- Because we want to 'hate out' at everyone.

- Because we are in denial of the true accountability of eating.

- Because we want 'time out' from life.

- Because… because… because… and there are many.

2. We eat because of our file from the 'filing cabinet' and the belief we have that food is 'love', rather than for its nutritional offering.

3. We eat because we think food gives us what we need, the metaphorical hug', and because we have no idea how else we can give ourselves this hug.

Associative Eating

1. Whilst driving a car.

2. Whilst watching TV.

3. After being outside and we come in to the home,

4. Because it's Friday.

5. Whilst having a drink.

6. With other people… etc… etc… etc.

There might seem little difference between habitual and associative eating, and to be frank there are similarities. However, with the associative eating there is usually some other defined object that kicks in the need to eat, for instance, the TV, a drink, a particular chair, and so on.

Although this book is more about facilitating an appropriate awareness of self and about providing the facts that cause our obsession with food and eating it, I think it would be remiss of me not to provide some suggestions we can take that could make all the difference.

There is no doubt that even with this greater awareness we are baffled with the difficulties we have not just to go out and change it all.

We still resist and hold ourselves back from change.

We are so used to being the 'victim' and having that extreme 'Borderline Personality', which implies not having any choice and going with other people's ways.

To be in that independent place does face us with a whole new set of ideologies.

Taking one step at a time we can see what holds us back and think of some solutions.

- Lack of the skills that enable us change

- Worry, thoughts, and anxieties

- Emotions.

- Indecision

- Environment

So let's go through these in greater depth to find our resolutions:

Lack of Skills

Let us remember the exercise where we looked at our behaviour of holding back on saying anything, in the belief that if we did there will be confrontation.

We think we do not have much conscious ability to know what to say or indeed how to act.

Predominantly we still accept the Critical Parent's 'should' and will impose that on how we change.

So when we look to change we will be saying to ourselves, 'How 'should' I do this? What 'should' I say? This is the crux of the battle!

Answer

There is no 'right' or 'wrong' way to 'be'.

Although we feel quite empty when we are left with just ourselves and let go of others peoples idea's and the Jackanory Theme we impose on others, we also have just ourselves to please and be aware of, and life is actually a lot simpler.

We are so disconnected from ourselves that when we listen to ourselves, our immediate response is to say we 'don't know'! Our reaction is to become scared and to panic that we will not get it right. Relax: we do know ourselves, and this transition will be fine.

Our way is neither the right nor the wrong way; it is our way, and it is OK!!

So communication–wise, how do we get this across? As previously mentioned, we say things such as:

- 'I would like….'

- 'I think…'

- 'I am not sure…'

- 'I am a little worried about…"

-
- 'I am feeling sad….'

We own our thoughts and feelings, and share when the time is right and with the appropriate person or people.

We will not eat.

Worrisome Thoughts

We have already introduced worry into the arena. However, by keeping calm and taking control, we can act effectively because acting effectively is what we want to do. So what are our worries actually about?

- Bad consequences. For example, others will think we're stupid.

- Whether we deserve to get what we want. For example, we are such bad people we do not deserve to get what we want.

- Will we be effective enough, or will we then leave ourselves open to name-calling. For example, 'You really are so stupid, what a mess you've made of that.

Answer

For this we need to look at the Underlying Beliefs previously mentioned. We do not want to act unsociably and to the detriment of others – that only occurs when we are the Rebellious Child and have done too much of the Adaptive Child.

When we are left alone and can have clarity in our lives, we will often want to live in harmony with others. This is what we need to think!

'Stupid' is a judgement call; it is a harsh measure we apply to ourselves and sometimes to others.

If we accept who we are and that we have our own needs and wants that are different than others, these worries – which are held in our Jackanory Theme – will greatly lessen.

We will not eat.

Emotions

- The feeling of guilt when we do something for ourselves can be huge – in fact there is a roller coaster of emotions: guilt, fear, frustration, anger. And let us not forget, we are not used to allowing ourselves emotions so this becomes scary too.

- Every time we have felt any emotion in the past we have eaten to dampen it, if not to numb it completely, so this is a whole new territory.

Answer

We need to tell ourselves we are emotional human beings and that to feel these emotions keeps us safe and allows us to live.

We will always emotionally respond appropriately.

If we allow ourselves these types of responses we will not 'blow up', and we will not harbour feelings that distort our mental state. Often, we think that we have let go and ignored the feelings and the thoughts we have around situations. How untruthful can we be? We store them and allow them to affect how we move on in life. Never, never do they go away if we push them down.

We will not eat.

Indecision

Being unable to decide what we want for ourselves in situations produces vulnerability.

- Do we really know what we want? Are we undecided about what the priorities indeed are for ourselves?

- Asking for too much when we have been so used to asking for nothing.

- Saying `no` to things as opposed to giving in to 'it all', all the time.

Answer

As we 'shift', it is normal that we start at one end of the spectrum, at one extreme, and travel to the other extreme, but in time we will move into the middle, where we are more able to recognise what will really benefit us.

If we can voice that we are undecided. The indecision can sometimes sound unreal, so as we hear ourselves speak, the thoughts we have can gain a greater clarity and in themselves move us to a stronger position. Once again, try communications such as these:

- 'I'm not sure if this feels right.'

- 'I'm a bit sceptical about....'

These type of sentences will embrace us and...

We will not eat.

Environment

This could be the most difficult factor, as there will always be times when the wanted outcome, or what we so want for ourselves will not come to fruition. For reasons such as:

- Other people are just too, too powerful.

- Other people will feel threatened by us, and will be unable to accept us and/or our decisions.

Answer

We need to recognise the therapeutic meaning of 'boundaries'.

This book looks at boundaries, the invisible fences between ourselves and others.

Boundaries free us from taking things so very personally. They enable us to accept that we are who we are, whilst others are who they are.

What we do is what we do is our business, and other peoples' responses to what we do is theirs and will be a result of their own up-bringing and life experiences.

Other peoples responses are their own, we might not like them, we might feel very uncomfortable with them, however we have no 'right' to shut them down or change them. At the point where we feel the need to do just that we are silently telling them that how they have responded is not 'right' and we are trying to change their response to fit in with our own agenda.

All of this is far too enmeshed, far too confusing and a 'recipe for disaster'.

Allowing each and everyone as well as ourselves their own agenda is a 'boundaried' place, a free place and a happier place.

The reason ultimately for this to be the case is because the 'boundaried' place has respect, for the self and for others.

We will not eat.

We always have choice. Always, always, we have choice. We might sometimes have to choose from a set of choices that we did not want in the first place, because others have changed them, but we must always see that we have choice.

What do I mean by this? For example, it is a nice sunny day, and we want to go to the seaside with the family. The other half – the husband, the partner, what you will – does not want to go particularly, but will if forced. Immediately, we can feel let down, and that we never get our own way, and that the partner always gets his, and that we never have choice.

But we still have choice. OK, the set of choices of when to go and where to go have altered slightly, or at least are not the first things to think about. The first hurdle has been knocked down, but we must still keep going.

Choice. So we can go with a moaning partner, or at best a silent unhappy one, or we can let go of the idea, and think of something else that we both might want to do with the family. This way we are happy – because it is important to us that everyone is happy – we know that if we go to the seaside we will become cross having this slothful partner with us.

It is nothing to do with us that the partner does not want to go in the first place. He is allowed not to want to go; he is a person in his own right with his own needs and wants. No doubt, the 'shoe will be on the other foot' at sometime in the future, and when it is, we do not have to go for another person either.

Boundaries enable us all to live together with freedom and respect. In the Transactional Analysis model of Eric Berne, Adults have boundaries and along with these there is respect.

Other people might be so wilful that they won't give us what we need. They might even involve themselves in attempting to punish us. However, we must know that we always have choice, Always. So we can either stay and be punished, or look after ourselves and go.

Once again, we must reinforce to ourselves that we have choice; a victim thinks differently, so this really does take us out of that place.

Being aware of how we physiologically react to situations can be a good anchor for us. It gives us an awareness of ourselves, as well as a real presence in situations. There is hardly anyone that is not aware of feeling uncomfortable, not aware of how the stomach muscles tighten. We begin to breath differently and even sometimes 'go red'

This awareness is enabling, and if when we go through these physiological changes, we can harness a certain type of reaction we take the choice to look after ourselves. An example might make this clearer:

Someone asks us a question that produces feelings of discomfort. To take control, we might like to say, 'I am feeling really uncomfortable around that question. Let me take a minute to sort myself out.'

Or if we go red, we might like to bring that into the open and say, 'Oh look, here I go, going red. I'm not comfortable with _____. Give us a moment to let the body calm down, and we can then talk about it.'

We will not eat.
When we do not share ourselves and yet have a reaction both emotionally and intellectually to a situation or indeed to life then it will almost always culminate in inappropriate eating. The eating might be caught on the back of something such as TV in the evening or sweets in the car but the seed has been sown from the emotionally 'disturbed' moment experienced earlier in the day or week or even

month, Because 'it never goes away' and we never forget not form an emotional point of view.

Whilst this book is absolute in its belief that the whole weight 'thing' is not about food, I also realise that there can be very definite benefits in having different thoughts and focussing on making specific changes when it comes to food. So for the finale, let us also look at the following simple rules.

What Can We Change When It Comes to Food?

Let us be very clear that there are two areas for us to look at when it comes to choosing different eating patterns.

- There is the area of food types and portions.

- There is the area of food behaviours.

So often in the past the whole job lot has been tackled; we have entered in the extreme place of absolute change in more ways than one.

This time we have to make it simple… because it can be simple.

We have to make it manageable so that we do not feel deprived and also because we are looking for a long-term way of eating.

We do not have to have this in the 'normal' struggle place that we live in.

Food Types and Portions

Let us call carbohydrates Yellow Foods:

- Bread

- Pasta

- Cereals

- Potato

- Rice

- Couscous

- Cake

- And so on…

Let us also see it as a fairly 'sloppy' food, because as soon as we have it in our mouths it turns into 'slop'.

However, Yellow foods provide the body and the brain with the energy needed to function properly and to be healthy.

Eating to burn fat requires that you learn to alter your carbohydrate intake; the trick to losing weight and weight management is to lower your carbohydrate for temporary periods of time, then raise them again, then lower them again.

In regard to Yellow foods, have them only once or twice a day.

The choice is ours as to *when* we eat them, the time is ours to choose, and the *type* of carbohydrate is also for us to decide upon, and we can vary it all through the week.

What we usually find is that if we eat the fuller meal at lunchtime, we do actually feel fuller for longer; we act in a more accountable way to the fuller meal and consequently eat less in the evening.

We have had the opportunity to use up the calorie content of the fuller meal too, because we have worked for the afternoon and into the evening.

The general sense of our physiology and our state of mind is that we have eaten, and we are satisfied and do feel pleasantly cosy and full. We act responsibly about the amount of food we eat for the rest of the day.

On the other hand, we might want to eat our fuller meal in the evening because that is when we are together with our family or spouse. Be careful of the possibility of distorted thinking. This might be an excuse we give ourselves to eat in the evening.

Often it is the case, however, that when we eat more fully later on in the day we will have the mind-set that we haven't eaten much during the day, so we over-portion our food.

We could also be reinforcing the famine and feast scenario; eating very little, if at all, during the day, and then with 'brownie points' in hand, whilst making the meal, the floodgates open, and we declare it our 'God given right' to make use of the brownie points gained in the day and so the feasting begins with only bedtime to stop it.

So with these basic foods we have choice. We want to lose weight. We can eat carbohydrates, we can eat them when we want, but the slight constraint is that we eat them once a day, because we **want** to lose weight. Having now read the book we can put into place the fact that if we really want to lose the weight it would not really be seen as a constraint but something we want to do!

As we become older, our metabolic rate does get slower; this might be a reaction to our doing less physical activity, or there could be other things in the mix. Maybe it doesn't matter why, but it matters that we are aware of it.

Although physical activity is helpful, this does not mean we have to go to the gym, as this would be an extreme, especially if we are at present doing nothing. We can eat vegetables that are slightly crunchy, and this assists the metabolic rate too.

Crunchy, complex vegetables use calories to digest and because of the nature of the work, the metabolic rate appears to benefit.

So I guess we would be looking at less Yellow, which results in less slop.

Can we make sure that we eat something crunchy of the vegetable type in quantity? This does not mean platefuls and platefuls, as we are always looking at the middle ground.

Naturally the protein foods can free-flow, but with the constant understanding that the body will not want for lots and lots of any food, and we are now listening to these messages given to us,

Eat the Real Thing

When we eat 'Weight Watchers' meals or other such diet food, we believe we can have more, because it has less calories or fewer carbohydrates, or less fat, or something.

Whilst these food types might have less of these food constituents the sugar and salt levels that are present is extra ordinarily high in order that there is some taste in the food at all.

When we eat the real thing, we can feel full because our body is aware of the fullness of the food, the ingredients being wholesome and not artificially 'bumped up'. From a psychological aspect we are more cautious and therefore more accountable because it is 'really what it is'.

Whenever we buy a 'weight watchers' anything there is always a sense of thinking it is less than what it is which brings in the thinking process of believing we can have more.

Once again then 'real' food makes us more accountable.

When it comes to portion size, only we know what we can eat, because we are the ones that know our output. Take into account the simplest of equations for weight management:

What we eat = our physical output.

I find it incredibly difficult to accept that various health spas and other such establishments believe they can make a plate that specifies the amount and the portion size of our food. Men and women are different. Output is different for all. Age must be brought into the equation too. These plates overlook all the variables that must be taken into account.

We need to learn by trial and error the amount we can eat. Once again, we must be aware of the pitfalls that might invade our thinking patterns, the distorted thoughts, the excuses etc which we are far more aware of now.

To be realistic let us look at the amount we eat now and the weight we are. So 'that' amount of food and that portion size gives us either maintenance of our extra weight or, at worst, it is increasing our size and weight.

Be careful here of any 'should' that might come to mind; it doesn't matter how small we think the portion size is. If this amount means we are able to lose weight, then it is the correct amount.

Often I have heard people tell me that that the amount of food they eat is nothing like it used to be and they wonder why their weight still increases. Leave the Poor Me place and become factual: if the weight is increasing, then the food portion is too big…. end of story!

Portion size needs to be determined by the individual; no one else can tell us because no one else knows our output.

- One Yellow food 'hit' per day.

- Have yourself some crunchy vegetables each day.

- Eat real food.

- Learn your own portion size.

Food Behaviours

This is an area that does not get a lot of attention. However, it is very important that we see it as a separate entity and as an area that can be changed with significant effect on our weight.

Behaviourally, are we famine and feast people? These are extremes, and we do hold extremes, so a lot of us probably are famine and the feast eaters.

With this in mind, we are able to see that breakfast is, therefore, a total disaster because as soon as we start eating, we very much want to carry on.

With every diet we have chosen to follow there has been the standard rule of 'breaking the fast' and taking breakfast. However, from the psychological aspect of 'all or nothing', we can see that this regime of breakfast is hopeless.

Drinking water in the morning is all it takes to break the fast and attend to the re-hydration necessary from sleeping through the night.

If it really does not suit us to eat as early as the morning, then we do not have to; if we did, we would be following the lead of the Critical Parent and being the Adaptive child to suit.

We must find out who *we* are with food, our being human, our humanness would suggest that we might not find the **ideal** solution as to how we live with food, but if we can find **a** way that enables us to manage our weight, then the larger battle is won.

And although the Critical Parent says we 'should' eat three meals a day, this is something we might not want to do.

Eat 'Instead Of', Not 'As Well As'

What does this mean?

- If we have to have the bar of chocolate, then have it instead of the dessert.

- If we have to have coffee with a biscuit, then have it instead of breakfast.

- If we are going out for a meal and plan to have a dessert when we usually do not, then miss breakfast that day.

- Allow ourselves a timeframe of 48 hours, and within that timeframe balance out the food consumption.

- If we like to pick at food in the evening, then do not have an evening meal.

- When we come home from work and have to pick, then do not have an evening meal.

It is probably not necessary for us to continue along the same vain, but the biggest step is for us to get out of the rut we have created for ourselves with food behaviours.

Being human suggests that we are not always in the same 'place' emotionally and psychologically every day, so why do we think that food-wise we are in the same 'place' every day I have no idea.

Many a lady I have worked with has shared how the food type and eating pattern changes at the weekend, because they can get up later and there is no work. So immediately we see how a change in the day can find us feeling and behaving differently, and so the food and the eating reflects this.

Why do we impose such rigidity around our eating otherwise?

If we are experiencing an incredibly stressful time or situation, and are really driven to feed into it, then so be it, but cut down on the routine meals, because we will not be hungry – we will only be eating meals from a sense of duty –and there really is no point because it will put weight on.

When the picking and the extra foods become acceptable because they are being brought into the balance, the meaning of eating them will change and the behaviour will alter, because we will not be `rebelling` with the eating, our Rebellious Child will have no effect and will then cease to want to `play` as often.

Always 'Balance Into' and Do Not Eat 'As Well As'

It is difficult to let go of all the old behaviours around food, but if slowly we can loosen their grip and be flexible, then we will find a pattern of eating that will eventually suit us.

As I say, it might not be ideal, but carrying extra weight is far from ideal. I guess this is about choice.

We are the only ones that really know the answers to our questions around food. We know our output and so therefore know what we can input.

- If we like 'heavier' foods, then we can eat smaller portions.

- If we like 'lighter' foods, then we can eat more of them.

Our bodies will tell us when they are full and when they are hungry; we just have to listen to them.

The body needs different types of calories to enter the body at each meal, because calories are like fuel, and to run efficiently, different types of fuels are what the body needs. This is done by changing the foods you eat at each meal:

- Protein

- Carbohydrates
- Fat

You don't have to worry about changing 'fat' calories, you only need to worry about the proteins and the carbohydrates.

Do Not Underestimate the Power of Water When It Comes to Burning Fat

Water suppresses the appetite naturally and helps the body metabolise stored fat. Studies have shown that a decrease in water intake will cause fat deposits to increase, whilst an increase in water intake can actually reduce fat deposits.

Here's why; the kidneys can't function properly without enough water. When they don't work to capacity, some of their load is dumped onto the liver.

One of the liver's primary functions is to metabolise stored fat into usable energy for the body. But if the liver has to do some of the kidneys' work, it can't operate at full throttle. As a result, it metabolises less fat; more fat remains stored in the body, and weight loss stops.

Drinking enough water is the best treatment for fluid retention. When the body gets less water, it perceives this as a threat to survival and begins to hold on to every drop. Water is stored in the extra-cellular spaces (outside of the cell . This shows up as swollen feet legs and hands.

Diuretics offer a temporary solution at best. They force out stored water along with some essential nutrients. Again, the body perceives a threat and will replace the lost water at the first opportunity; thus the condition returns soon.

The best way to overcome the problem with water retention is to give your body what it needs – plenty of water. Only then will stores water be released.

If you have a constant problem with water retention, excess salt may be to blame; your body will tolerate sodium only in a certain concentration. The more salt you eat, the more water your system retains to dilute it.

But getting rid of unneeded salt is easy – just drink more water. As it's forced through the kidneys it takes away excess sodium.

The overweight person needs more water than the thin one. Larger people have larger metabolic loads. Since we know that water is the key to fat metabolism, it follows that the overweight person needs more water.

Water helps to maintain proper muscle tone by giving muscles their natural ability to contract, and by preventing dehydration. It also helps to prevent the sagging skin that usually follows weight loss.

Shrinking cells are buoyed by water, which plumps the skin and leaves it clear, healthy, and resilient.

Water helps rid the body of waste. During weight loss the body has a lot more waste to get rid of – all that metabolised fat must be shed. Again adequate water helps flush out the waste.

Water can help relieve constipation. When the body gets too little water it siphons what it needs from internal sources. The colon is the primary source. Result? Constipation. But when a person drinks enough water normal bowel function usually returns.

To recap the remarkable truths about water and weight loss:

- The body will not function properly without enough water and can't metabolise stored fat efficiently.

- Retained water shows up as excess weight.

- To get rid of excess water you must drink more water

- Drinking water is essential to weight loss.

How much water is enough? On average a person should drink two litres of water per day, it can be water from the tap or still and it can be carbonated water.

However, the overweight person needs one additional glass for every two stone of excess weight. The amount you drink should also be increased if you exercise briskly or if the weather is hot and dry.

Water should preferably be cold – it's absorbed into the system more quickly than warm water, and some evidence suggests that drinking cold water can actually help burn calories.

When the body gets the water it needs to function optimally, its fluids are perfectly balanced. When this happens you have reached the turning point. What does this mean?

- Endocrine gland function improves.

- Fluid retention is alleviated, as stored water is lost.

- More fat is used as fuel because the liver is free to metabolise stored fat.

- Natural thirst returns.

- There is a loss of hunger almost overnight.

If you stop drinking enough water your body fluids will be thrown out of balance again, and you may experience fluid retention, unexplained weight gain, and the loss of thirst.

But to remedy the situation all you have to do is go back and force another breakthrough by drinking more water!

To burn fat your body doesn't pay attention to daily calories; your body pays attention to calories per meal, so spread them out as evenly as possible so that your body receives fewer calories per eat time. This allows you to burn fat… if you do this consistently every day.

Stop Eating at the Right Time

When is the right time to stop eating?

- Always stop eating before you are totally satisfied and whilst you are still just a bit hungry.

- Do not starve yourself; you do not need to leave yourself feeling 'very hungry'.

- Stop eating when you're still just a little bit hungry; this is really, really important.

- Every time you feel full, you are sure to add extra body fat to your body, because you will have given your body too many calories.

- Always try to make your meals as plain as possible. Condiments are loaded with mostly carbohydrates, which your body converts to fat tissue very easily.

- The difference between being fat and being thin can be decided by how many *plain* meals you eat. This does not mean every meal must be dry but use the sauces sparingly.

Eating Out – Simple Rules to Follow:

- Never eat pre-dinner bread" or appetizers.

- For pre-dinner salads, use vinegar-based dressings and not the creamy type sauces, and with no croutons or bacon bits, etc.

- Do not eat dessert after dinner, remember too many calories in the *one go* will gain weight, take home your dessert and eat it later maybe, or just don`t have one because you realise you do not WANT one because of the effect on your weight!

- Try to avoid rice and pasta, due to their portion size, because these foods are so calorie dense their portion if appropriately served needs to be a couple of table spoons and we all know they are way over that, instead get vegetables.

- Avoid breaded or fried foods.

- Always leave wanting a little bit more!

Understand that there is a difference between a Yellow food being unhealthy and being fattening. In other words, a food can be healthy but still be a fattening food.

There are many healthy foods that are loaded with important nutrients and have a low carbohydrate rating (glycemic rating), which makes them very healthy. However, these same foods are often calorie–dense, which means that our body cannot process all of those healthy calories, and so it converts the extra calories to fat tissue. It would seem that we are driven to eat large amounts of these foods as they are seen as our `snuggly` foods, but once again portion size is important.

I have known a few ladies that have put on weight really only eating foods we see as healthy, however their portion size of these foods was too big, healthy foods do not mean we can eat lots of them, we still have to balance or weight will be gained.

For example, pasta mostly is healthy; it has a low carbohydrate rating and is enriched with other important nutrients that your body needs. However, it is calorie-dense, which means that a typical plate of pasta has double the number of carbohydrate calories that your body can process.

If you want to eat pasta and stay slim, then you need to eat a portion approximately half of what you would expect to give yourself or receive from a restaurant.

Rice is the same.

So the question is not one of healthiness, but of calorie Density.

If you were on an island on your own with all types of foods and unlimited quantities and this was a long term situation the only measure you would have to understand the limitations of your food intake would be the body you have telling you how full it feels.

You would learn what foods gave you an upset stomach and what foods made you feel tired along with which foods gave you an energy boost. Eventually you would choose to eat the foods that gave you a better felt sense of self and it would be those foods that you would want to eat.

Your body has a lot to offer you
Your body knows how to take care of itself if given the chance.
Listen to your body and not your head!

And Remember...............

An Autobiography in Five Short Chapters
By Portia Nelson.

Chapter 1

I walk down the street.
There is a deep hole in the sidewalk.
I fall in.
I am lost... I am hopeless.
It isn't my fault.
It takes forever to find a way our.

Chapter 2

I walk down the same street.
There is a deep hole in the sidewalk.
I pretend I don't see it.
I fall in again.
I can't believe I am in the same place.
But, it isn't my fault.
It still takes a long time to get out.

Chapter 3

I walk down the same street.
There is a deep hole in the sidewalk.
I see it is there.
I still fall in... it is a HABIT.
My eyes are open.
I know where I am.
It is my fault.
I get out immediately.

Chapter 4.

I walk down the same street.
There is a deep hole in the sidewalk.
I walk around it.

Chapter 5.

I walk down another street.

Printed in the United Kingdom by
Lightning Source UK Ltd., Milton Keynes
139912UK00001B/118/P